THE HOT SEAT

THE
HOT SEAT

A Complete Manual of Rally
Navigation and Co-driving

STEVE FELLOWS

MRP

MOTOR RACING PUBLICATIONS LTD
32 Devonshire Road, Chiswick, London W4 2HD, England

ISBN 0 900549 90 4
First published 1984

Typesetting by Tek-Art Ltd., West Wickham, Kent
Printed in Great Britain by Netherwood, Dalton & Co. Ltd.,
Bradley Mills, Huddersfield, West Yorkshire

Contents

Introduction

Rallying is still the most exciting and enjoyable branch of motor sport. Once sampled it has a drug-like effect, drawing you further into the sport. Perhaps it is the unique formula of car, driver and navigator, who all have to contribute equally, which accounts for this strange compulsion. Or perhaps it is the friendliness of the sport which gives it a magical quality. Whatever, it is a sport which grabs your imagination by the throat, and which many, me included, find impossible to leave alone.

Writing this book has brought back many memories: good memories of the times when a near-perfect rally has brought the reward of an overall win, and bad memories of being stranded in the dead of night down some Welsh lane with a broken car, miles from anywhere, with the prospect of a long walk in pouring rain to fetch help. Strange, really, but no matter how many times you swear you will never do it again, you always turn up for another dose!

Traditionally, those involved in rallying always try to put something back into the sport. Retired competitors often turn their hand to organizing, passing some of their experience on to the newcomers. Others simply never give up! I hope that through this book I can give something back to the sport which has given me so much enjoyment over the years.

STEVE FELLOWS

July 1984

Acknowledgements

In compiling this account of a fascinating sport, my thanks for help should be a never-ending list. Every competitor and every marshal on the events I have tackled over the last 16 years has donated invaluable information. Every mistake made has taught me a lesson. Particular thanks must go to the drivers who have striven to test the nerves of this particular occupant of the 'hot seat': Dave Hartill, John Trevethick, Chris Beddow, Tim Harborough, John Farlow, Larry Potts, Geoff Birkett, Bill Gwynne, Peter Vaughan, Malc Graham, Ron Beecroft, Fred Henderson, Ian Tilke, Steve King, Ian Hughes, Cyril Bolton, John Lyons, Jussi Makunen, Bill Dobie and John Buffum. Thanks, also, to Ian Hughes, for the loan of a car to view the 'hot seat' from the other side of the fence and to the unyielding nerves of Alistair Roberts, for acting as guinea-pig navigator on that occasion.

My thanks also to Terry Harryman, for permission to reproduce his pacenotes; to David Sutton, for his service schedule; to Newtown and District Auto Club, for the information supplied on its Holrus Rally; to Caernarvonshire and Anglesey Motor Club, for permission to publish items from its Gwynedd Rally; to Hugh Bishop, Tony Large, Chris Ellison, Frank Williams, Nick Ford, Su Kemper and Mike Davies, for their assistance in researching and supplying photographs; and to Ordnance Survey, of Southampton, whose magnificent mapping is held in such high esteem throughout the rally world, for allowing the reproduction of examples of their Crown copyright material. My unending gratitude also goes to John Blunsden, for publishing this book and suffering the traumas of inevitably late copy. Lastly, to my wife Sue, for her tolerance, and to Gary and Emma, for taking notice of Dad's pleas for peace and quiet – thanks again.

S.F.

1

An Introduction to Rallying

A rally is not a race. Since the motor car was invented, there have been adventurers whose aim was nothing more than to out-drive others. They headed for the racing circuits of the time – little more than dirt tracks – where they pitched their motor car against others in a straight race. OK for some. Then they sought even greater adventure, turning their attentions to the open road – and the first rally had begun.

Great high-speed chases across Europe were organized. The French and Germans excelled, then the Alps were discovered as a natural testing ground for the fearless rallyists. Gradually, annual events like the Monte Carlo Rally became famous for both their sport and their social usefulness. The 'OK, yah' brigade would take the 'jolly old motor' down to Monte and come back with endless tales of daring-do to impress their society chums. Rallying was socially accepted and therefore a success.

But now, in the 'Eighties, the sport of almost millions has come a long, long way from those jaunty excursions of the 'Thirties. During the 'Forties and 'Fifties, the larger Internationals were simply for the driver. Thrashes around the countryside mixed in with sections of driving up grassy hillsides and sprints along seaside promenades. There were navigation rallies, more like treasure hunts really, organized no doubt to satisfy the needs of ex-RAF bomber navigators left over from the Second World War, but they were events more akin to a trigonometry examination than motor sports.

In the 'Sixties a revolution took place in Britain. At almost the same time, both club rallies and Internationals changed. Organizers of Internationals discovered how testing it was to send drivers into the forests. Jack Kemsley has been popularly credited with starting the trend with his RAC Rally when he found a pine needle in his Corn

Flakes one morning! Where else but in rallying could you expect to hear such a dubious tale, I ask you? Meanwhile, the club scene was shifting from the 'mathematician's delight' brand of event to what, at the time, was dubbed the 'Northern thrash' – an out-and-out race against the clock on public roads in the more deserted areas of the country.

Both caught on, and no wonder: the motoring enthusiast was being offered an exciting sport where he could brush shoulders with the best in machines which looked very much like his own everyday trasport. From a base in Europe, the sport spread East, West and South. Marathon rallies were held, stretching from Northern Europe to Australia and South America. The motor manufacturers were quick to see the potential in rallying as a marketing platform for their cars. Championships were organized, culminating in the present World Rally Championship, and professionalism came to the sport.

From its strangely humble beginnings as an activity sport, rallying has very much flowered into a crowd-puller. Our own Lombard RAC Rally regularly attracts spectator figures in the 2 million bracket. Yet it still remains a humble motor sport, where the lowly clubman can compete in the self same rally as the Hannu Mikkolas of the world.

What do you need to go rallying? Simply this: a car, a driver and a passenger who is prepared to brave all and guide his chosen leader in the right direction. The car in most cases can quite literally be anything on four wheels with an engine. The driver can be any man in the street with a need to satisfy his competitive yearnings, but the passenger, well, he's someone quite special.

Anyone can drive a car; it's something we do every day, isn't it? Anyone can even drive quickly, save the odd one or two little noisy periods which accompany

Road rallying is the starting place for most folk, where relatively standard cars can produce good results. Here is road rally champion Ron Beecroft on the 1983 Bolton Midnight Rally with John Millington burying his head in the maps. (*Ellison*)

brushes with the scenery, but it takes a modicum of intelligence to be regarded as an occupier of the 'Hot Seat'. Whilst it's not a requirement of brilliant academia to be a driver, the basic skills of reading and writing are pretty useful, although the more advanced skill of joined up writing may outstretch many of them. Not so with the passenger, my friend. He will not only need the wits of a scholar to out-do the devious amongst the rally fraternity, known commonly as the organizer, but he will also need the wile of a wizard to better the most devious of all creatures in rallying, his rival navigators or co-drivers.

Navigator or co-driver? Well, there are basically two types of rallying – road rallying and special stage rallying. Road rallying involves events traditionally held at night on public roads, where a driver and car are navigated, usually by means of a map, around a prescribed route. Certain of the sections are described as Competitive, where the organizers set a time and give penalties for exceeding that time. Other sections are called Non-competitive and are usually parts of the route which pass through villages or other populated areas. Certain rules are set down for organizers and the most important is a maximum

30mph average speed limit for competitive sections. Now, these days it's not difficult for a District Nurse in her Citroen 2CV to average 30mph down country lanes, so organizers tend to choose their rally route using very narrow and twisty tracks, festooned with tight bends and including myriad junctions.

It's the navigator's job to guide his driver safely and accurately down the route, using his maps to the full with the ultimate aim of reaching the finish unscathed and with the least number of penalties. What was that? Sounds easy? Well, just remember the old adage 'fools rush in . . .'.

Special stage rallies, on the other hand, rely on their Competitive sections which are run on private property. They mostly take place during daylight and have relatively straightforward and easy routes. They are very much a driver's rally and it's usually the man who can pedal his car the quickest over dirt tracks and unmade roads who wins, with little regard to the co-driver. But a co-driver who is also a navigator and a good 'office manager' can make the world of difference to a mediocre driver. The term co-driver is generally given to passengers on stage rallies, where the passenger would be expected to drive long, boring road sections, allowing the driver

After a spell in navigational road rallies many drivers turn their attention to special stage events. They offer greater competition for much more powerful cars and give the co-driver more to think about than is first imagined. Pictured is Colin Short in a famous Ford Escort RS tackling a forest stage rally in the South of England. (*Large*)

Who knows where it all might lead? The world of stage rallying opens up a huge variety of events, ranging from small club thrashes to adventures like this, the World Championship Ivory Coast Rally, where Guy Frequelin and Jean Todt drove this purposeful-looking Peugeot 504 Coupe. (*Bishop*)

to rest, ready for the next special stage.

There is traditionally a great rivalry between navigators and co-drivers, the former viewing their stage rally counterparts as 'sacks of potatoes', just carried along for the ride to satisfy rally rules. The more ambitious navigator will eventually end up as a co-driver and maybe he'll turn out to be one of the fortunate and talented few who make a name for themselves in international rallying.

The beauty of navigating or co-driving is that you need very little to make a start. Unlike a driver, all you need to buy is a map and you're away . . . and who knows where it might end?

RAC MSA General Competition Regulations

The RAC Motor Sports Association governs all motor sport in Great Britain and publishes its rules and regulations in a yearbook known coloquially as the Blue Book. It is essential that a good navigator knows his way around the Blue Book.

It contains rules for both organizers and competitors, and details vehicle restrictions. Any changes in rules are publicized in *Competitors News*, published at intervals by the RAC MSA. Changes to rules are first discussed by the RAC MSA Rallies Committee, which comprises members from every branch of rallying and is advised by Regional Committees, who in turn are advised through Regional Association member clubs. Once the Rallies Committee has agree rulings, they must be accepted by the RAC Motor Sport Council before they become motor sporting law.

Every Competition Licence-holder receives a copy of the Blue Book free of charge, along with copies of *Competitors News*. It is up to the navigator to correctly interpret rally regulations. Each event is governed by the RAC MSA yearbook rules containing the General Competition Regulations (GCRs) for competitions. Rallies are also governed by Additional Supplementary Regulations (ASRs) issued by their organizer – these are commonly known as the Regs for the rally. Any changes to the ASRs are notified to competitors in Final Instructions; from then on organizers can issue instructions during rallies by written Amendments.

2

Basic Navigating Skills

Having decided you possess a cast-iron stomach, an aversion to sleep and need a change from the universal Saturday night activity (there's always Sunday morning for that, anyway), rest assured, you are about to embark on a marvellously rewarding and adventurous new sport in rally navigating. But be warned at this stage. If you seek glory and admiration from your fellow mortals, forget it. As far as drivers are concerned, you – the novice navigator – are the lowest life form, a complete unknown quantity. You will soon learn that it's the driver who gets the glory, it's he who has the girls rushing to shower him with kisses when he wins, and it's he who gets the loudest applause at prizegiving as you are joined by the other 'left-hand men' huddled in a corner out of the limelight; but you have your own satisfaction. Thanks to your guidance and decisions, you've gained a result, and if you make a habit of it, the word will spread through the unique jungle telegraph system that is rallying. Your reputation will spread and you will find your outings will bring even better rewards until the right driver comes along and asks *you* to navigate for *him*. You will steadily build up an understanding with your driver and, before you know it, you are the flavour of the month in road rallying. Then *you* are in the enviable position of being able to pick and choose.

Starting out in rallying is simple. If you have a basic interest you will have heard about the sport from friends or by seeing it on television. The next step is to find a motor club and join it. A 'phone call to the RAC Motor Sports Association in London will help you to find your nearest club. Or try the specialist papers and magazines; they deal with motor clubs all the time and will soon be able to advise you about the best ones to join.

Once a member of a club, you will soon be asked to help out with its rallies. The most likely thing

you'll be asked to do is to stand out in some forest somewhere which will inevitably be bleak and miles from a pub. There you will stand religiously at the spot where a senior official told you to stand and you will wait for rally cars to hurtle past at breakneck speeds, but with an eye open for the safety of the approaching rally crews and any spectators who may be around. This sometimes thankless pastime is called marshalling, and without marshals there would be no rallying.

Having given you an initial taste for rallying, the next move is into road rally marshalling. Your club is bound to be involved with some small road rallies held on Saturday nights. Helpers are always needed, but it's not advisable to go blundering in without a bit of practice first. Find out who is going to marshal a control on the next rally and ask if you can come along, too – offer to supply a hip flask of something warming, that usually does the trick!

Marshalling in this way gets you known around the motor clubs, it introduces you to organizers and competitors, but most of all it shows you how rallies are run. But always remember one thing: rallying is fun and not the place for petty officialdom, so don't go mad with power just because you have a marshal's armband or badge – if you do you'll soon get a bad reputation and probably a black eye!

The mystery of this new-found sport will gradually unfold before you, and as you learn more, thoughts may turn to navigating on a rally yourself.

Navigating can start from very humble beginnings, like a Table Top Rally one club night, probably organized by one of the navigators in your club. They are ideal to learn about maps, how to find the rally route and the methods used to describe the route – and all within the confines of a warm clubhouse. Then there are Treasure Hunts, which can be anything from the 'OK, yah' Conservative

Marshalling can be the most thankless task in the world, as this official on the Codasur Rally in Argentina would no doubt confirm. (*Kemper*)

Club jolly on Sunday afternoon to a table top rally on wheels. After that it's into proper road rallying against the clock on Saturday nights, starting with small club thrashes and progressing to full-blooded championship rallies with other crews from all over the country.

Maps

Before anything else (even marshalling) you should know all about maps as the very essence of the sport revolves around them. In Britain, we are lucky to be in the enviable position of having what are arguably the best maps in the world. They are produced by Ordnance Survey, based in Southampton.

The most commonly used maps in rallying are the Landranger Series. In the days before we were all members of the European Economic Community, they used to be called one-inch maps, referring to their scale of one inch to the mile. They have now been metricated and are known as 1:50 000 maps, again referring to their scale (about 1¼ inches to a mile). They cover Britain in 204 different maps (called sheets), are extremely detailed and have the

National Grid marked on them.

The National Grid is a network of imaginary lines criss-crossing the country vertically and horizontally. The grid starts from a point in the Atlantic Ocean South West of Land's End, Cornwall, and finishes North East of the Shetland Isles. Now, by referencing a point in Britain (say your house, for instance) to the grid, a unique set of letters and numbers can be given to allow anyone able to read maps to pinpoint that place. Big deal, you might say, so can an address; but an address can't pinpoint a road junction, a certain bridge or a rally control.

This unique set of letters and numbers is called the grid reference. A grid reference is, however, a pretty unwieldy creation in itself, a typical one being SN 87100 91250. That pinpoints a place down to the nearest metre! The letters refer to an area 100 kilometres by 100 kilometres. The figures refer to the number of metres East and North from the 100km grid lines. They will be repeated every 100km, so unless the letters are used it is not a unique reference. In rallying, usually only three

Index to 1:50 000 Series

A total of 204 sheets cover Britain in the Ordnance Survey Landranger series of 1:50 000 scale maps. (*Crown copyright*)

figures of the grid reference are used. The last two (tens and units of metres) are dropped. That leaves 871 912, which can now be plotted on a map. All that is needed now is to know which 1:50 000 sheet to plot it on. Because these 100 kilometre squares need several sheets to cover them, it is usual to substitute the reference letters with the sheet number *e.g.* sheet 136/871912.

These Ordnance Survey 1:50 000 maps are being constantly revised with more up to date information and are issued firstly in Series, then in Revisions. When OS decided to go metric, its one-inch maps were simply photographically enlarged to fit the new scale and were known as 1:50 000 First Series sheets. Gradually they are being updated to Second Series sheets, being completely redrawn using slightly different symbols and colours. The OS expect all 204 sheets covering Britain to be totally upgraded to Second Series by 1990, so we're stuck with some First Series sheets for a few years yet.

Maps are produced from information gathered by surveyors using theodolites and tape measures, or by aerial surveys, where the ground is accurately photographed from the air. Both sets of information are put together using computers and a map is literally drawn on a piece of plastic film. This used to be done by hand, but now computer plotting tables have taken over.

Landranger maps include a key to symbols down the right-hand side, starting at the top with roads and paths, passing through general features and abbreviations with information about grid references at the bottom, along with revision details so you can tell just how old is the map detail. Right at the bottom of this column, on the left, is the revision letter (if the map has been revised). This is quite important in rallying, as the latest revisions are always used. The revision letter should be an 'A'. Further revisions will be shown by a '*', then a '-*' under the letter A and so on.

The map itself shows all roads in different colours according to their grade. Motorways are blue, main A roads are magenta (red on First Series maps), B roads are brown. Side roads and lanes regularly maintained by Local Authorities are show in yellow, with farm tracks and little used roads in white. Reds, browns, yellows and whites (as they are known in rallying) are shown bordered by a solid black line if fenced and a broken line if unfenced.

Grid lines (one kilometre apart) are marked in blue, with every tenth line slightly bolder than the others. Around the edges of the map are grid numbers, which are used for plotting map references – on Second Series maps these numbers are repeated on the map itself at intervals.

Some idea of the type of area covered can be found from contour lines (drawn in light brown).

These lines join points of equal height and occur at 10 metre vertical intervals. If the lines are close together the area is hilly; the closer they are the steeper the slope. Steep slopes on roads are shown by arrows printed over the road. A single arrow indicates a gradient between 1 in 7 and 1 in 5; the arrow always points downhill. A double arrow means a slope steeper than 1 in 5, which can make even a powerful rally car strain a bit when climbing it.

Time spent studying maps is fascinating and never wasted. They are packed with information, but surprisingly, few good navigators use them to their full potential. Find your nearest stockist and stick to him; trying to get everyone from your club to use the same shop is useful as well. If you keep in with him, he is more likely to help you out if you need a certain map in a hurry. Shops usually carry their stocks in folded, stiff-covered maps, but flat unfolded sheets are available instead (usually a bit cheaper as well). It's purely a case of personal choice, although the folded maps do tend to wear on the folds, but some sticky tape on the back or Magic tape on the front before you start helps them last a little longer. Always use maps that are in good condition – it's difficult to get a driver to appreciate that you couldn't 'call' the hairpin at which he's just rolled because there was a hole in your map!

TABLE TOP RALLIES
Having been bitten by the bug, table top rallies give the budding navigator a starting point to proper rallies. They may be simple, lighthearted club night puzzles set by a navigator, or they can be serious and complicated affairs, taking months to complete as the commercially available types invariably do.

These rallies use a 1:50 000 map and a multitude of different methods of defining the route. Because they all have an imaginary route, competitive dashes through the centre of towns and villages can be used, which would ordinarily be outlawed in real life. The more popular types of route plotting follow, with many rearing their heads again in other aspects of the sport.

Map references
Plotting by map references is the simplest and most straightforward way of describing an entire route. All that's needed is the right map, pencils, an eraser and a piece of plastic called a 'romer'.

A romer enables six-figure map references to be plotted accurately. There are many types on the market, all for around £1. One corner is divided up into tenths of a kilometre (at a scale of 1:50 000) along both edges and has the numbers 0-9 printed against the divisions. By sliding it on the map and matching up grid lines with these divisions, the required map reference point appears at its tip.

A piece of plastic like this is called a romer and allows map references to be plotted very accurately.

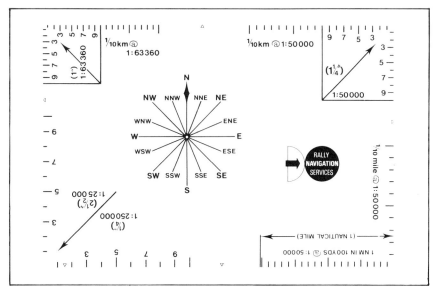

This diagram shows how a romer is used to plot the reference 598864.

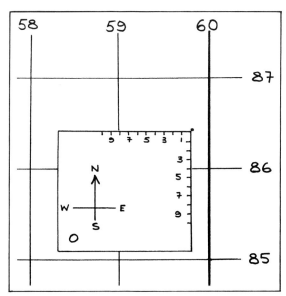

The simplest map reference appears as a group of just four numbers *e.g.* 6499. The first two numbers refer to the Easting (across the map) and the other two the Northing (up the map). These numbers describe a kilometre square on the map, extending East from grid line 64 and North from grid line 99. These are usually given by organizers to mark areas of Out of Bounds. Instructions that just the North half, or the West half of a kilometre square are Out of Bounds (or Black Spots) are quite common.

The most commonly used references are six-figure, *e.g.* 598864. The first three figures refer to the Easting and the other three to the Northing. To plot the reference, first find the grid line 59 running vertically down the map. Place the romer so that its figure 8 on the upper edge coincides with grid line 59. That moves the tip of the romer 8/10ths of the way into a kilometre square. Next, locate the 86 grid line running horizontally across the map. Slide the romer up or down the map until the last figure of the reference, in this case a 4 marked on the side edge of the romer, coincides with grid line 86. The tip of the romer is now at map reference 598864 and with the point of a pencil, mark a small dot on the map. The organizers will probably give a direction of approach (say South) or direction of departure (say East) to or from that point to define a route. As more are plotted, a route will be built up by joining together the dots.

Occasionally, and certainly where roads pass close to one another on the map, further accuracy will be required by adding 1/2 or 1/4 to the Easting or Northing. You then have to move the romer 1/2 or 1/4 of a division to find the reference point.

The golden rule when plotting a map reference is to mentally split the number into Easting and Northing, then plot the Easting (across) first. One of the most quoted little ditties to help remember this is: you must go ALONG the hall before you go UP the stairs. There are one or two more memorable quips, mostly concerning the female anatomy, but I can't mention them here!

Tulip diagrams
'Tulips' originate from the classic old Tulip Rally in Holland. They are 'matchstick' drawings of junctions, with a dot indicating the approach direction and an arrow head the departure. There could simply be a row of them, each describing every single junction along the route, or a distance between diagrams can be given, in which case you

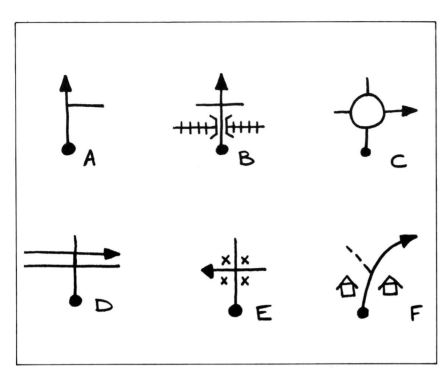

Tulip diagrams can be used to describe a rally route:
(A) ignore a road on the right. (B) straight on at crossroads after a railway bridge. (C) turn right at traffic island. (D) turn right on to dual carriageway. (E) turn left at crossroads with traffic lights. (F) bear right through houses ignoring 'white' on the left.

stay on that road until the next instruction. They can be used to distinguish between traffic islands and normal junctions, but usually apply to just coloured roads – 'whites' being shown by a broken line. Their most common use outside table top rallies is in defining special stage rally routes.

Herringbone

So called because it resembles the backbone of a fish picked clean by the local 'Tom'. The lines on either side represent junctions and, in a way, a Herringbone is a series of Tulips joined together. Like Tulips, 'whites' are shown as broken lines.

Looking at the diagram, the easiest way of using Herringbones is to think in terms of following a kerb. Junction A is straightforward, you keep straight on at a crossroads. Junction B can mean two things: miss a road on the left, or turn right at T junction. If you think of it as following the right-hand kerb it becomes clearer. So junction C could mean miss two roads on the right, or turn left at crossroads, but by following the left-hand kerb you can't go wrong. Junction D shows a white road included.

Unlike Tulips, Herringbones give no indication of the distances between junctions. Junctions A and B could be 50 metres apart, but junction C could be another mile down the road. Because of this, Herringbones always show every single junction, so the map has to be studied very carefully.

Some organizers with a sadistic streak in them join both ends of a Herringbone together to form a Circular Herringbone. Very often a starting point on the circle is not given, so it's a trial-and-error exercise until you get it right. These, thankfully, are dying out – so are their originators!

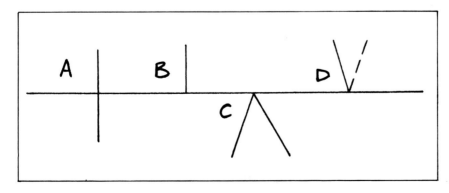

A typical Herringbone diagram.

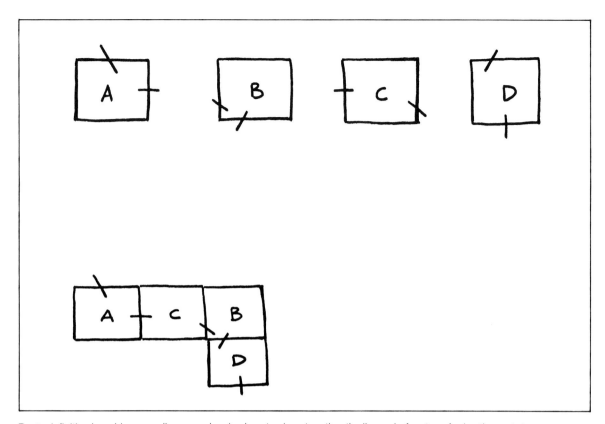

Route definition by grid square diagrams showing how to piece together the jigsaw before transferring the route to a map.

Grid lines
These are usually a string of numbers which have to be split into twos. They then refer to grid lines to be crossed in that particular order. Sometimes just a string of numbers will be given with no further instructions: the catch here is that some six-figure map references may be mixed up in with the numbers.

They may also be depicted as diagrams of kilometre squares with marks where the route crosses them. They will be given in no set order, so the first thing to do is establish a starting point, then piece together the jigsaw of squares before transferring the route to the map.

Spot heights
Looking at a 1:50 000 map very closely, minute black dots can be seen scattered along roads, with black printed figures nearby. These are spot heights, with the figures giving the exact height of that point above mean sea level. Routes can be defined by listing the values of spot heights to be passed through in a certain order. When no order is given, it is best to circle all the spot heights in pencil before joining them together.

Tracings
A drawing of the required route may be given on a sheet of tracing paper. The start point may be given, but by trial and error it will be quite easy to pinpoint the correct route even if you are not told where it starts or finishes. Transferring the route to the map invariably means destroying the tracing because of the need to push a pencil through it every now and again to make a mark on the map below.

TREASURE HUNTS
A treasure hunt is something like a crossword puzzle on a map. They are usually held on a Sunday morning or afternoon, finishing at a pub or club. You can be given different route instructions to follow, with clues to find along the way, or you can be told where the first clue is and from there, each clue tells (in a roundabout way) where the next can be found. Obscure things like numbers on manhole covers can be used to make up map references, or numbers on railway and canal bridges can be used. Nobody ever takes them seriously – they're just good fun – but with your wife or girl-friend driving, it lets you get a little more accustomed to reading a map on the move – and to know what the various symbols mean by relating the map to your surroundings.

3

Road Rallies

Road rallies generally take place at night, when country roads and tracks are almost deserted and when headlights can give a warning of oncoming traffic. Everyone gathers either at a garage or car park during the evening, then receives route instructions before heading off into the country lanes at about midnight. Depending on the type and grade of event, the route can be a 60-mile half-nighter finishing at a garage at 2 or 3am, or can last until just before dawn, covering over 150 miles and finishing at a hotel where a hearty breakfast can be eaten.

Cars are usually fitted with more powerful lights, sumpguards to protect the engine's vitals when driving down rough and rocky tracks, and good, full-harness seat belts. Some enthusiasts prepare their cars specially for rallying, tuning engines for extra power, fitting wider wheels with special tyres, and gutting the interior to save weight. Others simply turn up in their usual road car or their wife's shopping car.

There are grades of rally to suit everyone and every pocket, ranging from a local club '12 car' to a Restricted-status championship event.

All rallies have to be organized to comply with certain rules and regulations issued by the RAC Motor Sports Association, whose offices are based at Belgrave Square, in London. Rally organizers must have a permit issued by the RAC MSA to run their events legally, except in certain circumstances when a waiver of permit can be given. Organizers have to send copies of their planned route to the RAC MSA Route Authorization Department, along with a timetable of their rally. The same road cannot be used more than once every six weeks, so as not to annoy any residents, and an average speed of 30mph applies throughout the rally.

From time to time, the RAC MSA changes its rules governing road rallying, the most recent of these coming into effect on January 1, 1980. The biggest alteration was to simply split road rally routes into Competitive sections and Non-competitive sections. Competitive sections are the meat of the event, where the pressure is on to drop as little time as possible. Non-competitive sections are where drivers have to travel slowly and not use powerful lights, either because the route passes through a village, or uses a main road for more than half a kilometre.

Rally routes include a number of controls, manned by marshals. The organizers issue the locations of these controls on what is called a Route Card. The organizers also give each crew a Time Card, which the navigator hands to the marshal at each control and is eventually used to calculate their results. Crews are penalized for visiting controls late or for not visiting them at all.

The officials

Although the RAC MSA governs the sport, it empowers other officials to run each individual event. In road rallying, the rally boss is the Clerk of the Course. Sometimes he appoints a deputy to take some of the weight off his shoulders, but generally speaking it's all down to this one man to be responsible for the entire rally. He is usually a regular competitor himself (probably a navigator), invariably above such earthy measures as bribery, and it's he who invents the route. He will map out his ideal rally route, then send it to his area Rally Liaison Officer, who checks it with the local Police for suitablility of roads and areas where the residents are known to be 'anti-rally'. When a route is settled, it is passed to the next man down the line to gain approval from the RAC's Route Authorization Department. That man is the Secretary of the

RAC-appointed Scrutineers carry out checks for compliance with RAC MSA Vehicle Regulations and general roadworthiness before each rally. (*Ellison*)

A typical scrutineering bay on a small club rally – as long as it keeps the weather out nobody minds a few unpainted walls! (*Ellison*)

Stringent noise checks are made before cars can be allowed to start night-time navigation rallies. The noise meter is placed a fixed distance from the car and checks the sound level in decibels as the car's engine is revved at 5,000rpm. (*Ellison*)

Meeting and he has the task of dealing with a mountain of paperwork and forms required by the RAC. Then there is an Entries Secretary, who receives competitors' entry forms and fees.

A Chief Marshal is found and he recruits Sector Marshals, who in turn ask, press-gang and generally 'persuade' enthusiasts to turn up on the night and act as marshals. There may be half a dozen sector marshals for an event, each responsible for their portion of the route. The RAC lays down rules about visiting local residents along each road used by the rally (called 'PRing') and it is usually the sector marshal who does this personally, sometimes having to knock on a hundred or more doors to inform them of the rally passing by and to ask if they have an objection. Even though no-one can legally stop a rally passing by if a route has been authorized by the RAC MSA, who act as a Government Agency, it is considered a basic courtesy to visit each household – there could be someone living there who is ill, in which case the rally would be re-routed to avoid passing that particular house.

Competing cars have to pass through a noise check before each rally, so a noise Judge of Fact can make sure they comply with RAC Vehicle Noise Regulations. A Scrutineer is appointed to check the cars' roadworthiness and compliance with more RAC Vehicle Regulations.

A Results Team is formed to work out the competitors' penalties at the finish. There may also be a Timekeeper to look after the valuable clocks that are issued to marshals. Judges of Fact are needed to make sure competitors observe certain rules and a Driving Standards Officer is there to see that all competitors behave themselves and obey basic traffic laws. Finally, there are the Stewards of the Meeting, who are there to see fair play by all and to write reports of any official protests made to them by competitors, which are then forwarded to the RAC. Stewards are always well-respected figures in rallying, having been top-class organizers or competitors themselves, so they know all the tricks, and should be treated accordingly!

The rally route

This is what sorts the men from the boys. A good one is the pride and joy of every Clerk of the Course; a bad one can take years to recover from. They can range from the simple straightforward use of yellow and white roads to complicated affairs with tricky control sitings and using every road in a very compact area.

There are several governing factors which restrict the organizers to using only certain areas of some maps. The lack of alternative roads is the obvious one, especially in desolate moorland regions where it may be necessary to include a section of grass track to link parts of the route. Apart from this natural problem, there are a whole host of official restrictions imposed on rally organizers by the RAC MSA and the Police and, of course, the feelings of residents along the way are taken into account.

Known areas of 'anti-rally' feeling are listed as Black Spots by the RAC and are freely available to motor clubs. These Out of Bounds areas have arisen because a resident has made a substantial complaint about rallies passing his house and has made an official approach to his local Police Force. In some cases the rally organizers have been at fault in not 'PRing' their route properly, but in most cases it's just a perpetual moaner who is best avoided for peace of mind. The sign of a good organizer is one who re-visits residents after the rally has been held; in this way any ill-feeling can usually be settled on the spot and may stop a Black Spot being created.

Villages and towns can also restrict the choice of routes, although it is possible for a rally to pass through a village quietly under supervision of a Judge of Fact. The time of year can also affect the choice of roads. A farmer who is delighted to watch a rally pass his barns and fields in the autumn, will certainly not welcome a motor club during the lambing season when his sheep could be disturbed.

The availability of a suitable rest halt halfway through the rally for cars to take on petrol has to be taken into account, although few rural garages refuse the opportunity of selling so much fuel, even if it is at 3 o'clock in the morning! Then there is the biggest factor: proximity of another event in the area.

As mentioned earlier, the RAC MSA has ruled that no road can be used more than once in any six weeks, and it takes good liaison between motor clubs to clear that hurdle. Sometimes a club may be based 100 miles from the area in which it intends to run its rally, so good contact with the club whose patch the route runs through is essential and can save many wasted hours of planning. It's no good an organizer charging on blindly with a route, only to have it returned by the RAC Route Authorizaton Department because another club has used some of its roads a couple of weeks earlier. This can cause bad feeling between clubs when one organizer has pinched all the best roads for his rally, leaving the other starved of territory, but generally it's a case of 'share and share alike' and the fortunate organizer will usually give the other one first choice the next year.

All these factors have to be taken into account in the route planning stage, but little thought is given to them by competitors. Their main interest is in plotting the correct route and staying on it to the finish. Although there are instances of other methods of defining the route, by far the most common is by six-figure map reference.

The location of controls to be visited, and usually the direction from which they are to be approached, are listed on a route card, which is handed to each navigator before the start. The RAC rules state that no routes can be handed out more than two hours before an individual crew's start time – this stops enterprising navigators arriving at the start early, plotting the route, then driving over part of it to check for hazards or short cuts. The two hours is a maximum time, so organizers may hand their routes out later, giving the navigator less time to plot and introducing a 'panic factor' even before the car leaves the start. These are all called pre-plot rallies and they make up the bulk of road events, although some take place in parts of the country where the roads are of a less taxing nature – East Anglia for instance – where an organizer keeps the navigator on his toes by issuing the route as the car actually starts. This is called 'plot 'n' bash', and the navigator has the unenviable task of plotting the route as he goes along, whilst keeping his driver on the right road at the same time. These rallies have to be very carefully organized, as less experienced crews tend to wander from the pack and travel down roads that are off route, which can cause havoc with PR work if several crews make the same mistake and travel through a Black Spot.

The rally route is defined in two ways: Out of Bounds areas (Black Spots) which have to be avoided, and map references which have to be visited in a certain order. The correct route is always the shortest distance between points. The equipment you will need comprises:

Romer. That's the little piece of plastic used for plotting map references. It's best to hang it around your neck on a long length of string – apart from singling you out as a navigator, you always know where it is in a hurry. It also allows you to add drama to that moment when, in keeping with tradition, you ceremoniously lift it off over your head, signifying retirement from the rally! If your romer has more than one scale, it's a good idea to cut off the unwanted ones, so you can find the all-important 1:50 000 corner easily. If it doesn't have the points of the compass marked on it, draw them on; they are vital in moments of confusion for finding the correct direction of approach.

Pencils. Use soft leaded ones (preferably 2B) to give a good black line and make it easier to erase, but avoid pencils softer than 3B as they tend to smudge. Have about half a dozen, so if one breaks, you don't waste time having to resharpen it. Even better, try to get hold of a clutch pencil, one which takes fairly thick leads, and again use 2B, but steer clear of propelling pencils as their leads are far too thin to show up boldly enough in a bucking rally car.

Eraser. It's a foregone conclusion you will make a mistake in plotting, no matter how good you are! You therefore need to erase the error. Choose a soft pencil eraser because the hard ones will make mincemeat of your maps very quickly. The best ones are plastic erasers used by draughtsmen, which seem to virtually soak up the pencil mark, leaving the map unscathed.

Map board. Used to rest the map on. It needs to be about 18in square and made from cardboard (anything stiffer could give you a nasty stomach injury in an accident) and it's a good idea to cover the back with thin foam rubber to stop it sliding when resting on your lap. A couple of big paper clips are useful for attaching the map to the board, although some navigators favour the map to be loose. However, clips are also useful for attaching the route card to the board; that way you always know where it is and you are bound to need to refer to it at some time during the rally.

Map light. A fairly powerful car interior light (a reversing lamp is ideal) is a useful aid to plotting in a dark car park before the start. Or, fit one of the commercially available 'flexilights' which can be bent into position to illuminate the map.

Map magnifier. For reading the map on the move, this is essential. Commonly called a 'Poti', after a well-known make of magnifier, there are several different types available. All are illuminated and some even have rheostats which can be used to dim the light, keeping a useful boost in reserve for those eye-straining moments towards the end of a long, hard rally. Many also have a scale visible through the lens to help judge distances better when magnified. The genuine old Poti has part of its body cut away, so a pencil can be poked through to make a mark on the map without moving the magnifier out of the way. It is generally a case of personal preference as to which type you choose; they all cost between £10 and £20, but a quick look around a rally start will soon show which is the most popular.

That is basically all you require in the way of hardware, so now it's on with the job of plotting the route.

Black Spots are plotted on the map first, usually because that is the first information an organizer gives you, and as it is not actually defining the route, it's not governed by the two-hour rule. They are normally given as four-figure map references (one kilometre squares) with details of whether it is the whole square or just a half or a quarter, *e.g.* 9565 North half or 9565 South West quarter. These kilometre squares will usually blot out a town or village and may be a few miles from the intended route. If the Black Spot is nearer the rally route, it will generally be given as a six-figure map reference, together with a radius in metres *e.g.* 954652 300m radius. Alternatively, you could be given a list of six-figure map references and told that roads through those points are Out of Bounds.

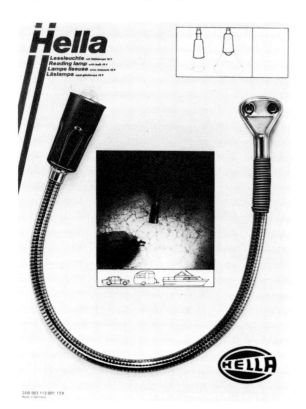

Flexible lights like this are invaluable in providing a powerful concentrated area of illumination which will not be distracting for a driver.

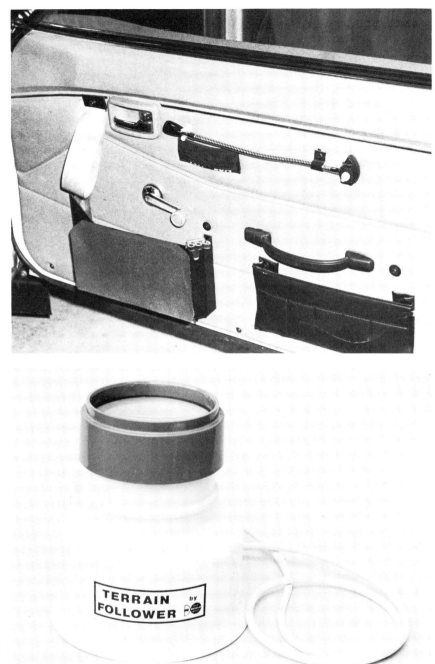

Door pockets are always useful additions to any road rally car; here an extra door pull handle has been fitted as well, together with a neatly fitted flexible lamp. (*Bishop*)

Map magnifiers come in all shapes and sizes; it is simply a matter of personal preference as to which one you should choose.

Transfer the information to the map by firstly marking the outline of the area with a thick line. Then hatch in the area with diagonal lines, but never completely obliterate the map – if you get completely lost and have to revert to the ultimate disgrace of stopping to study signposts, a village name hidden under a thick covering of 2B pencil won't help your cause. Similarly, if a certain road is Out of Bounds,

simply put a thick cross through it. On the rally itself, avoid Black Spots like the plague – no matter how strong the temptation is to use one as a short cut. The penalty for going Out of Bounds is exclusion – no argument! Incidentally, if you retire from a rally with a broken exhaust, don't take a short cut home through a Black Spot – to the public, you are still a rally competitor and if the RAC gets to hear of it,

Out of bounds: Km square 115/6268

| | | | | Time | |
Cntl.	Reference	App.	Dep.	allowed	Instructions
MTC1	115/5827222½	–	W	–	Start. Quiet Bangor.
TC2	6497223½	NE	–	12	Non-competitive to TC2.
PC3	620¼691½	NNE	–	–	Give way 620¼691½
TC4	617678	NNE	W	12	Give way 617678, 612677
TC5	594707	E	W	9	Non-competitive to TC5
					Give way 583709
PC6	573½682	NE	–	–	Give way 560½691½, 539½682
PC7	543½680	NW	–	–	Give way 545½662½

This example of a route card from the J.J. Brown Memorial Rally shows the controls listed down the left-hand side, followed by the map reference. Directions of approach and departure are listed next, followed by the time allowance for each section. Finally, a list of instructions is given to cover such things as Non-competitive sections, Give Way junctions and cautions. It is all translated to the Ordnance Survey sheet illustrated on page 27. The Non-competitive section from MTC1 to TC2 is shown marked with a broken line, whilst the section from TC2 to STC4 is a timed-to-the-second Selective and so is shown by a double line. Give Way junctions are circled and marked with an 'S' for stop. (*Crown copyright*)

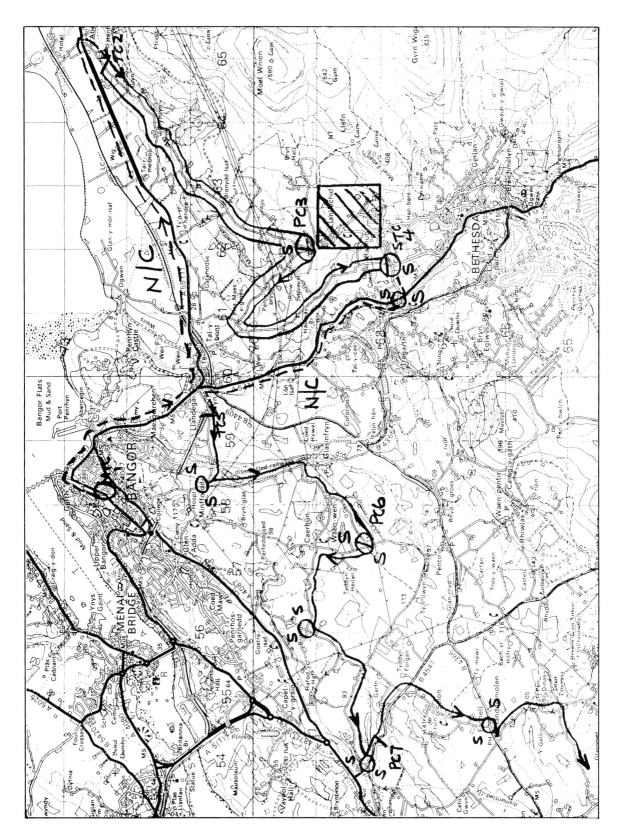

they may come knocking on your door and asking for your Competition Licence.

Some organizers take pity on navigators and put the list of Black Spots in order, so you work systematically down the map, whilst others jumble them up in an attempt to needle you straight away, meaning you are switching from the bottom of a map to the top constantly – and even from one map to another. If several maps are used, the organizer may prefix the four-figure reference with the map number, or he might just leave you to sort it out yourself. Always watch out for maps which overlap each other, and be sure to transfer all the areas in the overlapping section from one map to the other – sometimes organizers won't repeat them, taking it for granted *you* will.

With Black Spots plotted, the next on the list is the route itself. Consisting of Competitive and Non-competitive sections, you will be required to pass through controls (either time or passage) with marshals on duty; visit certain points called 'vias' (in defining long sections where the proper route may be unclear, you will be told to pass from one control to another, 'via' a certain map reference) which may not necessarily have a marshal on duty; and you will be notified of all junctions on the route considered to be Give Way junctions. Under RAC rules, all cars must stop at junctions governed by a standing Give Way sign, at a junction given by the organizers as a Give Way, and at junctions of minor roads on to A roads and B roads. Give Way junctions may also be included in the route card between controls indicating they apply to that particular section only.

All this information will be laid out in table form on your route card. The Black Spots may be repeated at the top of the route card – you should always check through them again quickly in case a new one has been craftily slipped in at the last minute. Lightly cross through references, or tick them off, once they have been plotted; this helps to keep your place on the route card.

If a list of Give Ways is given, they should be treated in the same way as a list of Black Spots, marking each clearly on the map before marking the route. The organizers may throw in a few red herrings, so don't assume you must pass through every single one of them. Give Way junctions will be given by six-figure references and will need to be plotted using a romer. Firstly, find the reference point on the map, then circle the junction in pencil, writing 'stop' or 's' next to it, but be careful not to write across a road which might turn out to be rally route, as you'll only have to rub it out later.

Generally speaking, the route card will list controls in a column followed by their respective map reference. Next will be a column for direction of approach, indicated by N, S, NW, SSE etc. That

may be followed by a column for direction of departure, but these are not always given. Then there should be a column for the time allowed for each section, followed by a column listing any relevant information. The latter would be used to show where to drive without auxiliary lights, or would give the reference of a hazard (known as a 'care') such as a bend with a bad drop on the outside of it, or a particularly rough stretch of track. When dealing with any information transferred from the route card to the map, it is best to tick it off so that, when you have finished, you can see at a glance if you have inadvertently missed anything.

The task of plotting the route can be eased if you can enlist the help of someone to read the references to you, but they must be trustworthy. It's no good getting a friend of one of your rivals to do it – a mysterious mistake will probably occur – so your driver is the obvious choice, and he will have a vested interest in getting it absolutely correct as well! If all else fails, then it will not take much longer to plot on your own.

The references can be read in two ways. Taking 247185 as an example, you must, of course, remember that the Easting comes before the Northing, and that you plot across before up. One method is to split the six numbers mentally into Easting and Northing, then plot the entire Easting first, as described under Table Top Rallies, followed by the Northing. So you would read 247, then 185. The other method is to split the reference further, taking the first two numbers of the Easting and Northing together, to give you the kilometre square straight away. Then you read the tenths and use the romer to find the reference point. So you would read 24, 18 first, then 7 and 5. The latter method is quicker, but until practised it could lead to more mistakes in splitting up the reference. In both cases, be very careful with complicated references like 711113 or 232323. You won't regret any time spent practising to plot references and it's a good idea to borrow some old route cards off your friends. You should aim to be able to plot two references a minute to start with.

Methods of marking references on to maps vary according to personal preference, but you should try to keep it simple. Once you have established a control point on the map, draw a short line across the road. Next read the direction of approach and mark a small arrow in that direction so that it touches the control line, then write beside it the control number, making sure it doesn't obliterate any information on the map. Plot the next reference along the route in the same way, then join the two together with a bold pencil line along one side of the road, carefully following the twists in the road, but don't draw it too close to the road. Never cut across the road with your

This navigator is well catered for with a flexible lamp, tripmeter, foot brace bar, spare romer and map magnifier. Plotting the route in a car is not the ideal place as you are bound to be disturbed by the inevitable 'door opener'. (*Ellison*)

pencil line, stick to one side or the other between controls. Sometimes a control will be sited at a previously marked Give Way junction, so if you stick to circles for junctions and lines for controls there won't be any confusion.

Plot the entire route, using just one line to define which roads to use. Once you have done that and find you have some time to spare, you can elaborate a little. Most novice navigators find it helps psychologically to have lines on both sides of the road. That's fine; go ahead and do it, but first things first – make your highest priority marking the route down in full. After all, it's no use leading your class up to the last control you've plotted, only to park for 10 minutes whilst you plot the rest of the route just because you wasted time at the start drawing two lines on your map when one would have done. That's the easiest way to have your driver reaching

for a jack handle or something equally as bulky with which to attack you!

Establish a set of route markings and stick to them, so you know at a glance which section is Competitive and which is Non-competitive. Some navigators mark Non-competitive sections with dotted lines, and Selectives (sections timed to the nearest second instead of the nearest minute), with a double line one side. It may also be helpful to mark direction arrows at intervals along the route, so that if your attention is diverted from the map (like pulling the car out of a ditch after your driver has suffered a touch of the 'heroes'), you know which way you should be travelling around the route. As with Black Spots, always duplicate the rally route on all overlapping maps. Study the route before you start and if there are any tricky junctions or places where the route loops back and passes very close to a previously used junction, make a larger and more detailed sketch in pencil to one side on a clear portion of the map.

Reading the route

Your driver is not asking too much when he expects you to do more than simply tell him which way to turn at each junction. To begin with, however, you will find even that is no easy task, and it is no joke when novices write 'L' and 'R' on the backs of their hands, for in the heat of the moment it's an easy mistake to make!

Right from the start, train yourself to keep the map upright on the map board. That way, if the road you are following through your magnifier is traversing up the map, left is left and right is right. When the road turns to run horizontally, it is relatively easy to orientate your mind to distinguish between left and right, but oh boy, use a road moving down the map and all hell's let loose; left becomes right and right becomes left – all very confusing. If you quite categorically can't cope with it, then start turning the map around so you are always travelling up it. It will mean you always know which way to turn, but you'll soon find just how cumbersome maps can be inside a car. Moving them around will disturb the driver's concentration, and any confidence he has in you will go right out of the window!

Orientating yourself to the map is the most important factor in learning a good navigational technique. Imagine you are looking out of the car windscreen as you follow the map. That farm track marked going off to the left; imagine you are actually looking at the entrance to it through the windscreen. Keep that up for a few miles and you are well on your way to a successful rally. With experience you will find that by studying the map you build a very accurate picture in your mind's eye of what lies ahead on the road. The map is a valuable fund of information; find the key to unlock its secrets and you have success on a plate.

When you have mastered the difference between your right and left, it's time to start thinking about passing information from the map to your driver. Exactly what information he needs is up to him. Some drivers need little help, just relying on the navigator to warn him of 90-degree bends and junctions, but others need their hands held very tightly, demanding you almost go as far as calling out every cat's eye!

When reading the road, accuracy is surprisingly not too important. You may describe the left-hand bend you are approaching as a '30 left' (bending about 30 degrees from the straight-on position), but your driver may know it better as a '45 left' (a bit sharper). If, however, you call another couple of bends the same, your driver will realize you are consistent and adjust his driving to suit. Similarly with judging distances, keep them consistent, even if they are constantly out by 50 metres. In judging distances, it helps to use one of the magnifiers with a scale visible under its lens; the scale need not be accurate, but it will improve your consistency. A driver will quickly gain confidence in your navigating if you are consistent.

Use farm entrances and other junctions as landmarks, especially on long straights or feature-less roads. It's no use simply telling your driver there is a '90 right' at the end of the one-mile straight you are on – the odds are he hasn't a clue how far one mile is! It's far better to look for a landmark near the end of the straight, enabling you to tell him, say, it's 200 metres to the '90 right'. Try to keep something like 400 metres or a quarter of a mile as your greatest measure; a driver can cope with that. If you do tell him it's straight for a mile or so, keep reminding him of the approaching bend at approximately half a mile, then 400 metres; it's amazing how quickly a driver can forget an instruction when he's concentrating hard.

The same goes for junctions. If you are on a fast stretch of road, keep reminding him he is looking for a junction, and if it's a tricky one, tell him to slow down in plenty of time. It's better to lose a few seconds looking for a 'slot' than to overshoot it and have to reverse or, worse still, go sailing blindly past it. When calling out junctions, always say 'turn' if it's a slot you want and 'ignore' if it's one you don't want. It helps your driver if he knows the severity of the junction and whether it is on to a wider road or a narrower one. If you are on a 'yellow' and turn into a 'white', tell him before you get there. Junctions between yellow roads could well be marked by a signpost, but slots into 'whites' might be simply a gap in the hedgerow. Always tell him what type of junction it is. A crossroads is straightforward, but be careful with T junctions to begin with. Tell him it's a T junction only if you are travelling up the shaft of the T; if you travel along the cross of the T, then it is simply a slot to the left or right.

Learn to study the map closely and, although this sounds obvious, tell the driver of every single junction, because a mistake at a junction means a wrong slot and could lead to your getting completely lost. Say you're travelling along a wide yellow road and you call out a '90 right' near a farm. Look at the map again and you might see a small track joining on the bend. That instantly turns your bend into a junction, so tell the driver. If you are not sure, then you can always say 'maybe a junction'.

Never give your driver too much information at once, his little brain box has its limitations and most of the grey matter will be reserved for concentration in keeping the car on the road; he can only allow a small portion for storing instructions. On most roads it's just a case of 'bend – straight, bend – straight', so keep your instructions simple, referring to the next bend only. Tell him the severity, direction and distance to the following bend – all in that order. When he has negotiated that corner and the lights have picked up the next, repeat the operation. By doing this, the driver knows the severity of the corner that's just ahead of him, but more importantly, he knows whether there is a good straight on the other side, allowing him to adjust the car's speed better – if he trusts you!

When corners are grouped closely together, don't bother to call the distances between them; you will find that a simple '30 right – 30 left – 45 right . . .' is enough, otherwise, the driver will soon be way ahead of your instructions. When you are approaching a series of twists, especially after a fairly quick flowing section, give him ample warning to adjust his speed and style accordingly.

When approaching a control, give plenty of warning and say whether it is a time or passage control – the latter will need the minimum of time-wasting. Also say whether there is a stop at a Give Way junction approaching, even if it coincides with a control. If the control is sited a few yards from the junction, don't forget to stop at the junction as well as the control! At Give Way junctions, ignore the beckoning motions of any spectators, there could still be a Judge of Fact waiting around the corner to book you, so always stop. Just before you grind to a halt at controls, tell your driver which way to leave the check point, even if the next junction is 200 metres away (the same goes for what bends are coming up) as it will take you a few seconds to find your place on the map after having to deal with the marshal.

In bad weather, a navigator is worth his weight in gold. He can help his driver immensely by warning of potentially slippery roads near farms when it's raining, or counting a driver down to a junction in fog. When there is a danger of ice, always tell your driver of bends well in advance; he won't be able to slow down as quickly as he would on a summer rally with nice dry roads. Wise navigators always inform of gates and cattle grids which have solid and unyielding posts either side of them. They are sometimes marked on the map as a thin black line across the road, but whenever the road edging changes from solid to dotted, it's a fair assumption that there will be some kind of temporary barrier there. Gates should always be open; it is a requirement of the RAC that they be manned as well, but there is always the exception and it has been known for a gate to be closed on following competitors by an enterprising crew. If you stumble across a closed gate, make sure you close it after you, unless your conscience tells you otherwise!

If you catch another car on a rally, never stop reading the road; the fact that you've caught them up should tell you they are not as good as you. It's a pretty idle navigator who takes a breather while his driver follows the tail of the other car – he may follow it right past a junction you need to take or, even worse, into a bad bend leading to the same inviting ditch. If, on the other hand, you are caught, tell your driver straight away the nearest possible place to pull over and let the quicker car through – farm entrances and junctions are ideal. If it's a non-competing car you've caught up with, bite your tongue and sit behind it on dipped headlights at a reasonable distance. The other driver won't welcome a mirror-full of powerful driving lights and it's a fair bet he won't pull out of the way, so just wait your time and be courteous.

There are three final points to remember on all road rallies. Firstly, never 'bull' your driver. If you are unsure of what lies ahead, tell him just that, don't try and guess because you will inevitably be wrong! Secondly, make it clear to your driver that he is in control (or should be) of the car at *all* times and should drive within his own capabilities, even if the '45 left' you call turns out to be a hairpin right – incidently, if this unfortunate situation ever does arise, be sure to congratulate your driver on his car control afterwards; appealing to his ego usually gets you off the hook! Finally, and most importantly, never forget you are on the public highway and that being part of a rally doesn't mean you have a God's given right to do anything you want – always respect other road users and be aware that there could be a car coming the other way down a narrow lane, even at 3 o'clock in the morning! To the uninitiated, rallying can be an awesome activity. So, be a diplomat for the sport at all times.

Controls

Controls are split into two varieties: those where times are recorded and those where simply proof of a visit is recorded. The former are called Time Controls and the latter Passage Controls.

A time control can be a main control at the start and finish, and usually along the route before and after a rest halt; a normal control along the route; a control at a Selective finish, where cars are timed to the second, or a control at the end of a Non-competitive section. At the start of the rally you will be given a time card. On it will be printed individual control numbers with spaces alongside for marshals to fill in the time, give their signature and possibly acknowledge that you approached from the correct direction. There may also be spaces reserved for official use by the results team. Guard the time card

TIME CARD   CLASS: A

CONTROL	APPROACH	SIGNATURE	HRS	MINS	SEC		FLS	MINS	SEC	CON
START		P.S	0	16				—		ST.
TC1N	✓		0	16				—		T1N
TC2	✓		0	17				1		T2
TC3	✓	Ge	0	19				2		T3
PCA	✓									PA
TC4	✓		00	23				4		T4
PCB	✓									PB
TC5	✓		00	23				—		T5
TC6	✓		00 30	03				7 03		T6
TC7N	✓		00	32				,		T7N
TC8			00 34					2		T8
PCC	✓									PC

This example of a time card from a Targa-timed rally shows a 1-minute penalty dropped at TC2, followed by a further 2 minutes at TC3, then another 4 minutes at TC4. The section to TC5 was cleaned, but 7 minutes 3 seconds was lost at the next control.

with your life! Without it, you have no proof of having visited controls. It is a good idea to clip the card to a board, so it gives the marshal a firm surface to write on. It is also useful to fit a marshal light to the inside of the car, positioned to shine light on to the passenger window. Many marshals fumble around with a torch, wasting valuable seconds, so by providing a light you will gain a speedier passage through a control. Making it foot-operated is also helpful when you have your hands full. If you don't have a special light, try positioning a ' flexilight' to do the job instead, but only use your 'Poti' to illuminate the card as a last resort – the place for that is firmly on the map covering your exact position.

The positions of all controls are given on your route card and, having noticed that each map reference can only be accurate to about 100 metres, their exact position is difficult to pinpoint. The RAC bypass the problem by declaring an area 50 metres in radius around the control point as the control area. Its boundary on the correct approach is marked by a control board (an example of which must be displayed at the rally start). You are said to have visited the control as soon as you enter the control area.

As you approach the control on the rally, have the car window open, with the time card clipboard resting on the sill ready for the marshal to enter his mark. You should tell the marshal what time you want (it may not be the time you get!) and your competition number, as the one stuck to your door will undoubtedly have become plastered in mud, making it unreadable. If it is a well-marshalled control, there will be two people; one will fill in the card, while the other will hold up the control clock for you to confirm the time. You are within your rights to demand to see the clock at every control, but unless you suspect an error, it's best to trust the marshal, otherwise you just waste more time. Don't hassle the marshals unnecessarily; it won't speed them up and they might be marshalling a second control later in the rally – and they will especially remember you as a troublemaker! If you do spot an error, ask the marshal to correct it, but make sure he initials the correction, otherwise the organizers could exclude you on suspicion of tampering with the time card – and make sure he marks the correction down on his check sheet as well. Most controls keep check sheets which are collected at the end of the rally and used to verify times in the event of someone querying them. They generally prove to be invaluable on a rainy night, when times become smudged on time cards.

Passage controls are treated in much the same manner, but generally all that you need to collect is a signature and no time. Some 'via' points marked on your route card could be manned, so if you see a control board, stop. A 'via' is usually treated as a passage control. If the organizers advise you that secret checks may be set up, tell your driver to stop whenever he sees a control board, irrespective of whether you mention it (because they're secret, you don't have prior knowledge of their whereabouts). These are used to check whether you have taken an obvious (and illegal) short cut, or have passed through a village quietly enough.

Sometimes an organizer is short of marshals. If he has planned for the eventuality, he will have told you that code boards will be in place at unmanned controls. It is then your job to write in the letter(s) shown on the board against the space on your time card – it is then usual for the marshal at the next control to sign the previous control space as well if you are correct (if he didn't, you should be able to cadge the letter off a friend at the finish). If, however, the organizer hasn't planned for an unmanned control, or perhaps the marshal's car breaks down on the way, you should just carry on to the next control, where you will no doubt ask, nervously: 'That last control wasn't there, was it?'. Hopefully, the reply will be 'No'.

Control boards have been known to blow down, so always tell your driver when you expect to approach one and he will look for marshals. Some dastardly marshals put up their control boards, then park just out of sight and wait for unwary crews to drive straight through without stopping – they are few and far between, thankfully, mainly because the pastime attracts too much physical violence towards them from aggrieved navigators! Code boards have been known to disappear, too, whether by natural or unnatural means.

At the end of the rally (and maybe at the halfway halt) it is up to you to find where the time cards should be handed in. If you don't, no-one will come running after you looking for them. Before you do, it's an idea to copy down your times so that you can check them against results later.

Finally, control areas are governed by strict rules. You can expect to be penalized for turning round in one, reversing into one, passing through one more than once and entering one from the wrong direction – although if you realize your mistake before the marshals see you, it's worth driving round to the correct approach and hoping they didn't spot your number first time round. You will also be penalized for arriving after a certain time and for arriving early.

Timing
Road rallying has moved towards a unique method of timing. It is an unconventional method, quite difficult to accept at first, but once understood it is simplicity itself to use. Known as Targa timing, it is a method where every control clock is purposely made

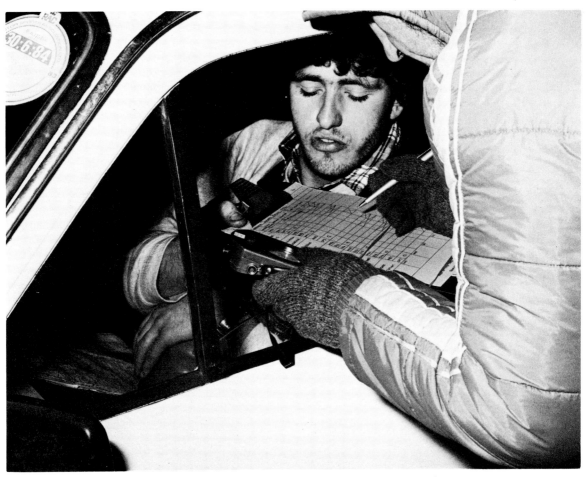

This marshal is well-organized, holding the control clock just where it can be checked whilst he fills in the navigator's time card. The navigator has clipped his cards to a stiff board and has this resting on the window to give a firm writing surface for the marshal. (*Ellison*)

to give a 'wrong' reading when compared with the standard time of day. In this way, the crew of a particular car on the rally should find that, if they maintain the proper rally schedule, the clocks will read just one time throughout the event. The name Targa is in deference to the old Targa Rusticana Rally, which first used the method back in the 1960s, and is the product of John Brown's inventive mind.

In rallying terms, the normal time of day you would have shown by a clock in your house or your wristwatch is called 'BBC Time' – after the Greenwich time signal transmitted by BBC radio. Now, because rally organizers have been known to bend the timing rules on road rallies, their control clocks would show up the indiscretions immediately if set to BBC time. That is one reason for Targa's rise in popularity, but by far the most significant reason for its success is its simplicity for the navigator.

The control clocks are set to run 'slow' in relation

to the rally start clock. Each section of a rally between time controls has a time set as a target to be aimed at by the competitor. If he makes it within the allowed time, he does not receive a penalty. Let's imagine the first three sections of a rally have been set a target time of six minutes, four minutes and four minutes, respectively. The rally uses Targa timing, so the competitor is due to arrive at every control with the same time showing on each clock, providing he is on time. To enable this to happen, the clock at the first control after the start needs to be set to run slow when compared with the start clock – in this case six minutes slow. The next section is four minutes long, so the clock at the end of the section has to be slow by an additional four minutes, if it is to show the same time as the start clock for a crew arriving on time. This is built up, control by control, for the entire event, with the cumulative total of section times to that point accounting for the amount that each particular clock is set slow compared with

34

the start clock. In this case, the clock at the end of the third section would be reading a time 14 minutes $(6+4+4=14)$ slower than the start clock.

Most organizers then take the simple step of relating the time shown on clocks to a crew's competition number, by adjusting the start clock to read a certain amount slow before setting the other clocks. It is customary for car number 1 to leave the start with the start control clock reading one minute past midnight – on a 24 hours clock read-out that is 00.01. Car 1 is then due at each control at 00.01, similarly car 37 is due at each control at 00.37, and so on. Most road rallies cater for around 90 cars and organizers generally take the step of simplifying matters further by giving the 60th car the competition number 100, meaning it is due at every control at 01.00. Piece of cake, isn't it?

Using the Targa method, working out time penalties is child's play. You simply subtract your competition number from the time in minutes shown at each control marked on your time card. But there is a snag. On all rallies you have to visit controls within a certain period of lateness, known as Maximum Permitted Lateness – this is usually 30 minutes. To find a particular crew's MPL time, 30 is added to their competition number (car 10 would have a MPL time of 00.40). That particular crew must arrive at all controls before this time, or they will be over Maximum Permitted Lateness and will have been deemed by the rules never to have visited the control.

On some of the tougher rallies, the road sections are extremely taxing and novices will soon find themselves dropping quite a bit of time, so organizers slip in a section with its timing relaxed enough for a novice crew to arrive at a control early. Under certain conditions, the crew can then book in early and reduce overall lateness, thus staying within their MPL.

In such a way, it is possible for a novice crew to amass a penalty of, say, 47 minutes at the end of the rally without actually exceeding their 30 minutes MPL. It sounds confusing, doesn't it? So let's look at the way the penalty system works.

Imagine you are a lowly novice running at number 110. You leave the start when the clock shows 01.10 (this is your 'due' time at every control), it is a five-minute section, but you wrong slot and arrive at the end of it after eight minutes. The time on the clock will be 01.13 – you have already dropped three minutes and collected a three-minute penalty. Each time represents two things – the finish time of the preceding section and the new start time of the next one, so your new 'due' time is now 01.13. This is because you cannot be penalized more than once for your time loss. That three minutes is now deposited in two 'banks', one accounting for penalties and one

for MPL. You arrive at the next control 10 minutes late, with the clock reading 01.23 (which becomes your new 'due' time at the following control). Ten minutes are added to your penalties account and to your MPL account. You arrive at the following control at 01.34 after another couple of wrong slots and a visit to a ditch! Not surprisingly, you are late, in fact 11 minutes late (due time 01.23, actual arrival time 01.34). This 11 minutes is added to your penalties, giving a total now of 24 minutes, whilst you are 24 minutes into your MPL of 30 minutes. Luckily for you, the next section is relaxed and you arrive at the control at 01.26, in other words you have beaten the falsely low target set for that section. You are now allowed to book in before your new 'due' time of 01.34 – the exact amount of time you can book in early is governed by strict rules which will be looked at later. For now we will assume you can book in at 01.28. You receive no more penalties, and your MPL account is reduced back to 18 minutes. Your new 'due' time is 01.28, but you arrive at the next control at 01.30 – two minutes late. The two minutes are added to both accounts, which now read: total penalties 26 (previous total 24, plus two more minutes); MPL 20. In this way it can be seen that your time penalties always accumulate, but your MPL account can fluctuate up and down.

A scale of penalties will be laid down by the organizers and these days they are more or less standardized. Arriving at a control late (arriving and departure are considered to be coincident) has a penalty of one mark per minute or $\frac{1}{60}$th of a mark per second if timing to the second is used. Not reporting at a control, and this means not arriving within your MPL or not approaching by the correct route, has a penalty of one Fail. So a novice who has run into trouble on the rally and booked in over MPL could have a total penalty expressed as 3F 47m 00s.

There are additional penalties for booking into controls early, usually double those of booking in late. These are to catch the unwary fast crews who may arrive at controls too early. However, booking in early is permitted in some cases. Under what is called the 'three-quarter rule', a crew can calculate exactly the amount of time they are permitted to arrive early. Every section of the rally has a time set for it, worked out on a 30mph average speed. However, the RAC allows crews to complete a section at an average speed of 40mph, which corresponds to three-quarters of the time set for a 30mph average. So for a 12-minute section, a crew is permitted to complete it in just nine minutes, in other words to book in up to three minutes early. This allows competitors to reduce their overall or MPL lateness, but it doesn't reduce the penalties they have already collected. Under the current rules,

Graham Evans checks his driver's times on the results board at a rally finish. Laid out in this way, it is a simple matter to check rivals' times for errors. (*Speedsport*)

if a section is set at four minutes or less, a competitor can book in as early as he likes without penalty (this is called 'making up time'). Having said that, though, a competitor can never book into a control before his initial 'due' time – his start time for the rally. So if car number 10 ever booked into a control before 00.10, he would be penalized for early arrival.

Competitors are allowed to enter the control area if they are too early, but must wait until the time they require is shown on the control clock before they actually book in – unless the rules for that particular rally say otherwise! Sometimes an organizer decides that competitors will be timed-on-sight by the control marshal, so that if you are early and wait in the control for your correct time, the marshal will

only give you the time at which you actually entered the control area.

Sections are generally timed to the previous whole minute, but to help in the event of two crews finishing the rally with the same number of penalties, organizers may time several of the sections to the previous whole second.

Timing to the previous whole minute means that if you arrive with the control clock reading 00.27.45, your time is regarded as just 00.27; the seconds are dropped. That gives you some leeway – 59 seconds in fact – but it also gives rise to some novices falsely thinking that the odd lost second doesn't really matter – it does! Say you arrive at a particular control with the clock reading 00.27.45, your due time is

00.27, so you are on time, but you have already lost 45 seconds towards your next time. That means for the next section, say a four-minuter, you no longer have 4 minutes 59 seconds in which to complete it, but only 4 minutes 14 seconds. So don't fall into the trap of thinking seconds don't count when timed to the minute, they always do. For this reason, it is important you tune your procedure at controls to a fine pitch. Watch an expert crew – they will stop for about 10 seconds at each control – then compare it with the 20 seconds taken by an ill-prepared novice. If there are 30 controls along the route, the novice will lose a total of five minutes more than the expert, just on slack control procedure.

Grades of road rally

Just like any other sport, rallying has a status ladder. As governor of motor sports, the RAC MSA requires newcomers to start at the bottom and achieve basic standards before being allowed to climb the ladder. It does this by issuing a Competiton Licence of the lowest grade (Restricted) to anybody who applies for one. To achieve the next grade higher (National), crews are required to finish a certain number of Restricted or lower-grade rallies; proof of this is provided by having rally organizers sign the licence as evidence of a finish. Then there is a similar requirement for upgrading from National to full International (the highest grade possible). You have to pay the RAC an annual fee for licences, which at the time of writing ranged from £8 for a Restricted to £30 for an International Competition Licence.

12 car. This is the lowest grade of competitive road rally and, as the name implies, it is restricted to just 12 competing cars. The RAC MSA waives certain requirements as far as paperwork is concerned, but apart from that it is a miniature road rally. These are normally short events where the only requirement to compete is membership of the organizing club. They are more likely to be a navigation type of rally, with different methods of plotting the route, rather like a table top rally, or they could be based on regularity sections. This is when an average speed is set for a section, *e.g.* 24.5mph, and marshals time competitors on sight. The controls are usually hidden around corners, so crews don't park just outside them and wait for their due time. A stopwatch and an accurate distance recorder are essential for these rallies – although there is more than one way of winning! The most common error is for crews to arrive early, so with early arrival penalties double those for late arrival, it actually pays to be purposely late. If in doubt, wait.

Closed (C). This status applies to a proper rally restricted to members of the organizing club. As many as 60 crews can compete and organizers might offer special rates for joining the club just for the one rally. Closed events are very few and far between, usually only one or two in each region every year. They are used as events for novices and beginners – your first rally could well be one of these.

Closed joint promoted (CJ). These are similar to Closed events, but theoretically are organized by several motor clubs. Only members of the organizing clubs are eligible to enter them. At this grade, events start to form the basis of club, or inter-club championships. They could include some 'plot 'n' bash' navigation and some regularity sections. The best CJ-status rallies offer excellent competition, although they do tend to have a strong local flavour. If you plan to travel to one outside your local area, expect to be fairly and squarely beaten.

Restricted (R). These events make up the bulk of road rallies and have to comply fully with all RAC requirements. These are the championship rallies, usually straightforward in navigation with pre-plot routes and without trickery from the organizers – they are the product of the famous 'Northern thrashes' of the 1960s, where a driver's capability was more important than a good navigator. As many as 90 crews can compete and clubs are invited to each other's rallies – in some cases Regional Associations of clubs (with 20 or 30 in each) are invited as well. To enter, you will need a Restricted (or higher) grade Competition Licence and a membership card of an invited club. There are unwritten grades of rally within the Restricted status, starting with non-championship events through regional championships to the tough and almost professional rounds of the *Motoring News/* BTRDA Championship, which attracts crews from all over the country.

Championships

As soon as you are reasonably competent, you should aim to compete for points in a championship. Start with your own club championship and work towards a regional series, moving on when you can afford the extra travelling costs to the nationwide events. This introduces a goal to aim for; without it you will just amble around, never knowing if you are improving or not.

Competing in a championship you will notice the same faces at each round and the events should all be of the same good standard – there is usually a healthy social atmosphere surrounding them as well. A championship can be a focal point for prospective sponsors, and reports of its qualifying rounds are generally given more space in the specialist motoring press than are non-championship rallies.

4

Your First Road Rally

The night before your first road rally you probably won't sleep. Your stomach will be knotted up with nerves while you turn over every expected catastrophe in your mind. Yet you will remember every single moment for years to come. But the story of your first rally really starts a couple of months before. For those who have yet to experience a road rally first hand, this is what to expect.

The rally detailed here took place in December 1983. Based in Newtown, Powys, the Holrus Trophy Rally was a Closed-status novice rally organized by Newtown and District Automobile Club. It had all the ingredients of a full-blooded road event, with a route that was straightforward, but over roads that would set an expert crew thinking twice in places. Here is a countdown of events which led to successfully completing the rally, starting eight weeks before it was held.

8 weeks. A casual chat during your club meeting leads to the suggestion that you should try a rally. You've already tried a couple of table top rallies and some treasure hunts and you have marshalled on four night rallies, so you feel the time is right to have a proper go. Your prospective driver has competed on half a dozen rallies and has only crashed once, so he's a pretty safe bet to start with. You look through *Motoring News, Autosport* and *Rally Sport* to see what rallies are coming up and find the Holrus looks a likely one – 100 miles on maps 136, 137 and 125, starts and finishes in Newtown, with an entry fee of £15, which includes membership of the organizing club. It's a Closed-status rally biased towards the novice, and with a class for beginners. Ask around your fellow club members and find out if some friends are competing as well – it's far better to tackle a rally with friendly faces around to help and guide you.

7 weeks. The Supplementary Regulations arrive and you carefully check through them section by section. On the inside front cover, the Foreword briefly describes the event. It states the route is on metalled roads, so it should be possible to use a standard car safe in the knowledge that there will be no rough, muddy tracks along the way.

The Supplementary Regulations (Regs) start with the announcement of the intended event.

1. This tells you the rally status, the type of rally (whether road or stage), the organizing club(s) and, of course, the date.
2. A standard clause detailing how the event will be governed. Note that a written instruction issued by the organizers during the rally has to be obeyed.
3. Another standard clause to show the event has been authorized by the RAC MSA and the Government. The DoE Authorization Number is rarely shown in the Regs as it is usually only issued days before the start, but it should be either notified in the Final Instructions sent to you just before the rally, or displayed on the Official Noticeboard at the start.
4. This tells you who is invited to compete on the event. Being a Closed-status rally, only members of the organizing club may compete, but if it was of Restricted status, there would be listed here the invited motor clubs and associations of clubs. It may also detail which championships it counts towards.
5. This details the entry requirements for competitors. In a Restricted event, it would state that a Competition Licence would also be required – if you don't have one, now is the time to apply for one from the RAC Motor Sports Association in Belgrave Square, London SW1.

6. A programme is laid out, giving you a rough idea of what time to arrive in Newtown.

7. This section is an important one for navigators. It shows which maps the route will cover and usually states the total mileage. It can detail the start and finish venues, and can be used to state if there are any timed-to-the-second sections. Also, the method of defining the route, *i.e.* by six-figure map reference.

8. Which class you should enter and each one's requirements are listed here. Pick your class carefully as the requirements do vary slightly from event to event. You may be a Novice in one rally, but a Semi-Expert in another. There is nothing stopping you from entering a higher class (except humiliation), but entering a lower class could result in the organizers penalizing you.

9. Some superstitious competitors skip over this section until they reach the rally finish. It lists the awards and on the bigger events you may be asked to nominate yourself for a special award on the entry. For example, a lighting equipment manufacturer might donate an award to the highest placed user of its product.

10. The entry fee is detailed, along with the last date an entry can be accepted – although some organizers can be pursuaded to accept a late entry, even though, strictly speaking, it's against RAC MSA regulations to do so.

11. The name and address of the Entries Secretary is shown.

12. The maximum number of entries is shown here, along with the minimum and the class restrictions. Organizers usually accept a number of reserves as well, to top up the entry if some crews don't make it to the start on time. Note that in this case it is a first come, first served basis of selecting entries – on some rallies the organizers select entries on a merit basis, particularly on championship events where registered competitors are given priority over others. Entry lists can fill up remarkably quickly for popular events, some within days of the Regs being published.

13. A standard requirement is for all the rally officials to be named. The various Judges of Fact may not be named here, but will be listed at the rally start on the Official Noticeboard. If telephone numbers are not given, it doesn't harm to find out how to contact the Clerk of the Course just in case you have any doubts about the suitability of the route – the Foreword stated all

---

NEWTOWN AND DISTRICT AUTOMOBILE CLUB LTD.

Foreword

Welcome to this years Holrus rally. This years event is aimed at the novice but also includes a class for the expert, who will also find it a challenging route.

The route will comprise approximately 100 miles in total, on metalled roads using maps 125, 136, 137. The entry fee includes membership of Newtown & D.A.C. Ltd., until 31st December, 1983.

If you are unable to enter, perhaps you could consider assisting with the marshalling on the night. Each control will be entered in a free draw for £5.

Acknowledgements :
The R.A.C. M.S.A.
The Dyfed Powys Constabulary
The West Mercia Constabulary
Bear Hotel
Marshalls, Officials and other helpers
All residents on route

NEWTOWN AND DISTRICT AUTOMOBILE CLUB LTD.

HOLRUS NOVICE RALLY

SUPPLEMENTARY REGULATIONS

1. The Newtown and District Automobile Club Ltd., will promote a Closed Permit Road Rally on 10/11th December, 1983 starting from Newtown.

2. The meeting will be governed by the General Regulations of the R.A.C. Motor Sports Association Ltd., (incorporating the provisions of the International Sporting Code of F.I.S.A.), these Supplementary Regulations and any written instructions that the organising club may issue for the event.

3. R.A.C. M.S.A. Permit Number RAL 1012/2 has been issued.
D.O.E. Authorisation Number . . . .

4. The event is open to all fully elected members of the organising club.

5. All competitors and drivers must produce a valid club membership card.

6. The programme of the meeting will be :—
Scrutineering starts at 20.00 hours
Individual times for scrutineering will be notified in Final Instructions.

Any competitor not signed on by 22.00 hours may be excluded.
First car starts at 22.45 hours.

7. Cars will start at one minute intervals.
Map numbers 136, 137 and 125 (1:50,000 series) will be required.
The finish will be at the Bear Hotel, Newtown.
The event will contain competitive sections on the public road, timed to an accuracy of less than one minute.

8. The event will consist of 4 classes as follows :—
CLASS A   EXPERT. Either member of the crew having been placed in the first ten of a restricted rally (or higher status) or in the first three of a Closed co-promoted Rally.
CLASS B   SEMI-EXPERT. Crews not eligible for Classes A, C or D.
CLASS C   NOVICE. Neither member of the crew having won any awards other then team, marque, or club award on any rally (other than 12 car).
CLASS D   BEGINNER. Neither member of crew having competed in any rally other than 12 cars.

roads would be metalled, but a last-minute change of route could include a muddy 'white'.

14. Notifying when provisional results are published is an important point. Most events publish the results at the finish venue, where there is a 30-minute 'protest' period for queries to be ironed out following the complete list of provisional results being displayed. After that time, the results become final and awards are presented. Some small events post provisional results to each crew during the week following the rally. There is then a seven-day protest period before results are final, but this is a 'messy' method, giving rise to confusion concerning protests and minor queries. If a postal system is used, it's imperative that a navigator keeps a close check on other competitors' times at the rally finish, so he can refer back to them when checking the postal results table.

16. Another important one for the navigator, it details when the rally route will be made available to them for plotting. If it's a 'plot 'n' bash' event, it will say so here. The 'L4.3.3.' and 'L4.9.7' refer to the relevent sections of the RAC Blue Book (RAC MSA General Regulations).

17. A note should be made of this section as it

won't be repeated in any other paperwork you receive. This one is straightforward, but some events state that large (12in) black numbers and a white background will need to be supplied by the competitor, to be placed on each front door of the car.

18. The system of marking is detailed with reference to the relevant section of the Blue Book. The letters listed refer to the sub-paragraphs of section L4.13.5. On some events a lower penalty is given for missing a passage control than for missing a time control. This is a handy point to remember if the going gets tight and you have to cut out part of the route to get back within your MPL. Note also the requirements to be classified as a finisher as these, too, vary from event to event.

19. Certain General Regulations can be modified by rally organizers and this section gives details of any such changes.

20. The timing system is detailed and explained. This event uses the customary Targa system.

21-24. These are sections of information only and are generally the same for every event.

25. Finally, if it's your first rally, you must arrange insurance cover – and the organizers'

---

9. Awards will be presented as follows :—

1st Overall	Driver : An award (Class A not eligible)
	Navigator : An award
1st in each Class	Driver : An award
	Navigator : An award
2nd in each class	Driver : An award (Subject to 5 entries in Class)
	Navigator : An award
3rd in each class	Driver : An award (Subject to 10 entries in A Class)
	Navigator : An award

10. The entry list opens on publication of these regulations and closes finally on 1st December, 1983. The entry fee is £15.00. All entries must be made on the official entry form and accompanied by the appropriate fee.

11. The Entries Secretary of the Meeting to whom all entries must be sent is :—
Miss Julie Evans,
Graylea, Pool Road
Newtown, Powys.
Tel. (0686) 26465. Note 6 - 7.00 p.m. only please.

12. The maximum entry for the meeting, including reserves, is 90. The minimum is 30.
The maximum for each class is 40.
The minimum for each class is 3.
Should any of the above minimum figures not be reached, the organisers have the right to either cancel the meeting or amalgamate classes as necessary.
Entries will be selected by order of receipt.
Entry Fees may be refunded less £2 for administration expenses up to closing date for entries. Refunds after closing date will be at organisers discretion.

13. Other officials are :—
Club Stewards. .Tony Hawkes, Roy Griffiths
Clerk of the Course . . . . .Keith Jones
Chief Scrutineer . . . . Harry Hockly
Chief Timekeeper . . . . .Hughie Hughes
Secretary of the Meeting. . . . . Martin Roberts

14. Provisional results will be published as soon as possible following the end of the event.

15. Any protest must be lodged in accordance with LI.14.7.

16. Entrants will be supplied with a Road Book/Route Card/Time Card 90 minutes before their due start time.
These documents will provide all the information nesessary to enable competitors to comply with L4.3.3., L4.9.7.

17. Competitors will be identified by rally plates which will be provided by the organisers : these must be displayed on the passenger door and rear of vehicle.

18. Marking and penalties will be as printed in the appropriate section of the R.A.C. M.S.A. General Regulations except as modified below :—
L4.13.5. Performances will be assessed using the 'Fail System' modified as follows :—

	Delete e, f, g, h, i, j, k.	
l.	Arriving at or departing from a control or check before due time	1 FAIL/MIN.
m.	Arriving late at a control	1 MK/MIN.
	For sections timed to less than ½ minute	1/60MK/SEC
n.	Early arrival at the end of a non-competitive section	1 FAIL/MIN
o.	Breach of statutory requirement concerning the driving of a motor vehicle, or failure to stop at Standing Give Ways and at Junctions specified as Give Ways in the Road Book	EXCLUSION
r - s	EXCLUSION BY JUDGE OF FACT.	
t	EXCLUSION AT FINISH SCRUTINEERING.	
u.	EXCLUSION.	

Classification for order of merit will be made from competitors who have incurred the least number of fails. Order of merit between competitors who have incurred an equal number of fails will be by reference to total marks lost.

If there is a tie the competitor who has completed the greater portion of the competition from the start without penalty or if both incurred penalties at the same point the competitor with the lesser penalty will be the winner. If a tie still remains penalties at subsequent controls will be taken into account before taking engine size into account.

To be classified as a finisher L4.13.1 and L4.13.2 will apply.

19. All other General Regulations of the R.A.C. M.S.A. apply as written except for the following which are modified :—
L4.10.8 The route will contain at least one section where timing will be to the previous whole second.
L4.10.14 All controls will open 15 minutes before the scheduled arrival of the first car and close 30 minutes after the scheduled arrival of the last car.
L4.10.24 Competitors may absorb any lateness incurred, at the refuelling halt and rest halt - however this is not mandatory.

20. Timing will be by Marshals clocks. Clocks will be so set that any one car will be due at every control at the same time, i.e. Car No. 1 will be due at every control at 00.01 and Car No. 7 at 00.07 etc. The 60th car will be numbered 100 and will be due at each control at 01.00.

timetable must be strictly adhered to! After being accepted by the RAC's brokers, Messrs C.T. Bowring, you will receive a letter showing what is called your RDS number, which should be quoted again on the entry form of future rallies. Once accepted into the scheme, you have no need to apply for cover again, but you must inform Bowring's of any changes in vehicle.

The numbers of individual paragraphs in the Regs may vary with each event, but basically the information is set out in this standard form.

The next step is to fill in the entry form and make out a cheque. It does no harm to start a record book of costs, which as you progress through the sport could be used to accurately predict costs for a season when looking for a sponsor.

6 weeks. You should receive acknowledgement of your entry from the organizers. If it hasn't come through, phone them up just to check they have received your form. If you have been late in returning your entry form and are told you are on the list of reserves, find out how near you are to the top. If there are more than 10 others in front of you, forget it and start looking for another event, then

---

---

write to the organizers requesting they cancel your entry and return your entry fee.

Once confirmation of acceptance has come through, it's time to buy your maps. Always make sure you have the most up to date revision of each sheet. If you don't already have them, buy some pencils (2B), an eraser, a romer and a map magnifier, and find yourself something to keep them all in, such as an old briefcase. You will need a map board and it's best to make one yourself. It will need to be about 2ft square, rigid enough to write on, but supple enough to bend in the case of an accident – if you go off, the last thing you want flying around inside the car is a 2ft square device capable of decapitating you and your driver! Try finding some corrugated cardboard and cover it with fairly thin card, then glue some thin foam rubber to the back, so it can rest lightly on your legs without slipping off. Get yourself a clipboard for holding time cards and you are kitted out with all you need to start navigating.

Ask some of your club's navigators for any old route cards they might have and start practising plotting map references and make sure you are confident about the method of timing being used on the rally. If you have a collection of old magazines or papers, or know someone who has, look up the reports of last year's rally to see if there were any problems – they could crop up again. Ask some of the more experienced navigators in your club if they have any information about the rally area that you should know about – there might be a particularly tricky area where the map is totally inaccurate. When asked, they will certainly let you copy down which white roads are OK to use and which just peter out. Unfold your maps and place some sticky tape over the back of the folds in the centre to help them last a bit longer.

4 weeks. By this time, your driver will be thinking about preparing his car for the rally and you should go along and offer to help with your side of the car. Make sure the seat is adjusted so you can rest your feet on something solid – even when tightly strapped in with seat belts, it helps to be able to brace your legs, giving a steady platform for the map board. Familiarize yourself with the seat belts. Know how to adjust them and how to get out of them in a hurry! Some experienced navigators prefer to use their own set of belts, transferring them from car to car. Choose belts with a wide shoulder strap, preferably slightly padded, and on the rally, keep them tight! Apart from the obvious safety factor, tight belts help to stave off car sickness.

Sit in the car, and with the belts properly tightened, make sure you can reach the window winder easily and, of course, any switches you have

NEWTOWN AND DISTRICT AUTOMOBILE CLUB LTD.

HOLRUS NOVICE RALLY 1983.   10/11 December, 1983.

FINAL INSTRUCTIONS.

Dear Competitor,

           We thank you for your entry for the Holrus Novice Rally.

Your Start No. is   -------------

Your Start Time is   -------------

Please Report to Noise Check Between 7.30p.m. - 9.30p.m.

Noise Check Reference 136/123920 (See Diagram).

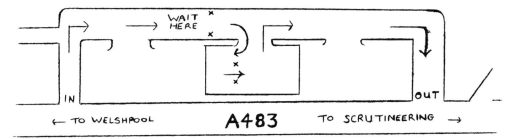

After Noise Check proceed to Start Area and fill up with Petrol.
Start Area Reference 136/120919 (See Diagram) Join queue for
Scrutineering then Park neatly in Area as directed.

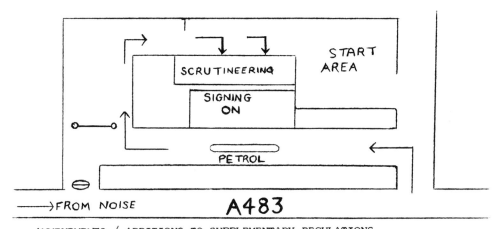

AMMENDMENTS / ADDITIONS TO SUPPLEMENTARY REGULATIONS.

Entrance to the Bear Hotel is from the REAR ONLY.
Breakfast will be available @ £2.00 per person.
DOE AUTHORISATION Number 18770 DE 10/11.
NOTE: Milage from Start to Halfway Petrol is 60 miles
No Petrol available at Finish.

to use. Good lights inside the car are just as essential as good lights outside. You will need a fairly strong light when plotting the route at the start. A small strip light (as used in caravans) is ideal, or a small square reversing light. Most people fit them above the rear-view mirror, but if they are fitted to the roof lining above the navigator's door they can double as a marshal's light. A small light with a flexible stem is a useful accessory which can be mounted out of the way, but swung into action when necessary – try to fit it close to where the map board will be, if your magnifier bulb fails it can be shone through the lens as a temporary measure.

Make sure you have somewhere to put your time card and pencils, etc. If there is no door pocket on your side, add one, or make a bracket on which to hang your clipboard. A box of chocolates should be enough of a bribe to encourage your favourite lady to run up a simple pocket with elasticated top which can be attached to the door trim if all else fails. A strong rubber band around the sun visor will keep pencils in place and readily to hand, along with a spare romer, whilst a length of stout sticky tape (carpet tape is ideal) will keep spare light bulbs and fuses in place on the dashboard. Always find a way of keeping things in their place; if not, by the end of the rally you will be convinced you are sharing the car with an unseen little creature which devours pencils, erasers and anything else which drops to the floor!

Familiarize yourself with the car interior, find out where the jack is kept, and learn how to use it. Practise changing a wheel, so you can work out a fast routine: navigator jacks up car while driver undoes wheel nuts; navigator fetches spare wheel and puts old one away (securely) while driver tightens wheel nuts; finally, navigator jacks car down while driver gets strapped in and starts engine. Carry some water repellant and keep it close at hand – it's your job to jump out into the water at a ford, whilst your driver tries to restart the engine, unless you can talk a spectator into doing it for you. They invariably won't help and it's then you realize they're not there to see the cars splash through, but to see the poor old navigators getting their feet wet!

1 week. Final Instructions will arrive, detailing your start number, the time you should arrive at scrutineering and your start time. Firstly, check through the entry list to make sure everything is correct. If you think you have been placed too far down the field, or if you know the crew directly in front of you is much slower than you are, then tell the organizers, but bear in mind you might not be the only crew with a grumble. If a higher placed car non-starts, the organizers could be persuaded to move you up into their place instead.

Check through the amendments (if any) and make note of any map changes. The DoE Authorization Number has been quoted, but the only alteration of any note concerns petrol. The organizers have stated that enough fuel for 60 miles is needed to start the rally, while there is no fuel available at the finish. Find out the location of the nearest garage on your route home and note the time it opens on Sunday morning. You may have to fill your car up at the halfway petrol halt, or wait at the finish until late on Sunday morning when a local garage opens – bearing in mind the rally probably finishes at about 3 o'clock in the morning.

The instructions tell you to visit the noise check first, followed by scrutineering, then to park up at the start. A map reference is given for both the noise check and the rally start, although in built-up areas, it is sometimes difficult to pinpoint a reference accurately from the map. The organizers generally include more detailed sketches of the start area, as they do in this case. Keep these Final Instructions, along with the Regs, in your rally case; the clipboard is a good place for the Final Instructions and entry list. Go through the entry list with your driver, singling out your opponents, ready to keep an eye on their times during the rally.

Night before start. Look at the maps again, have a good dinner, then try to sleep. Going to bed fairly late will help and it will delay a feeling of tiredness the following night.

Morning of rally. Treat yourself to a lie-in if at all possible. Have a good breakfast and gather all your equipment. Your pencils, etc, maps, Regs and Final Instructions should all be together in your case. You should take a warm, weatherproof jacket, and a hat is useful if you break down during the rally – a car can soon become very cold when stationary in the middle of the night. Pack some headache pills and something to drink, along with some biscuits and a couple of apples. A torch is pretty useful and you should always carry a spare romer and bulb for your magnifier, as well as a small screwdriver, along with some plastic insulation tape. A spare pair of socks isn't a bad idea, either, just in case you stop in a ford. Take a 1:250 000 Routemaster map of the area, to use if you find yourself hopelessly lost and travel off the other maps you have with you – one Routemaster map can cover the area of about 10 Landranger maps. All you then need is your money, Competition Licence and club membership card. Eat a hearty lunch – you might not eat again until early the next morning. Wear clothes you feel comfortable in, but leave the racing overalls to the special stage boys – it doesn't help the image of public road rallying to be seen wearing them.

Afternoon of rally. Arrange to meet your driver with plenty of time to load up the car and travel to the start. There is nothing more upsetting than arriving late in a flat spin. If you reach the rally start early, you can always find a cafe or pub for a snack, or spend your time driving over a few of the local roads, but slowly! If you are delayed and expect to arrive very late, contact the organizers and inform them of your problem, otherwise they will assume you are not planning to compete and will give your place to a reserve entry.

Aim to arrive at the noise check about 30 minutes early, allowing time to find it; it is usually tucked away on the outskirts of town or some remote place where revving engines won't annoy anyone. It is also an idea to find scrutineering before you need to as well. The next few hours will fly past!

18.30 hours. You arrive in Newtown on the main through road and find the start garage already bustling with people. Another half-mile down the road is a cafe, but first drive back up the main road to find the noise check site, which is still deserted. Now it's time for a coffee and a snack – you are not due at scrutineering for about another hour.

19.30 hours. Drive back up the main road to the noise check and join the queue. Watch a couple of cars being checked to see if there are any problems. When it's your turn, follow the marshal's instructions and your driver should gradually build engine revs to 5,000rpm. Keep the car windows shut, as some extra drumming noise from the car's interior could be detected by the meter. The marshal hands you a documentation card filled in with a signature against the first space: Noise Check. Keep the card in a safe place; you will eventually need it to exchange for your route card. Once clear of the noise check, ask your driver if he needs to adjust his driving lights and find a quiet stretch of road. While he's making the adjustments, check that all of your interior lights are working, including your magnifier.

20.00 hours. You join the queue for scrutineering and move forward into a service bay behind the start garage. The Scrutineer runs through a check of steering, brakes and all lights (particularly that your car's auxiliary lights automatically extinguish when the headlamps are dipped). He also checks that the front seats are secured so they don't tip forward and that a red warning triangle is carried on board. He will also check that the throttle has two return springs fitted – it's a good idea to carry a few spares in the car. When the Scrutineer is satisfied, he will sign your documentation card.

As you reverse out of the scrutineering bay, a marshal tells you were to park. There has been a problem, though. Some garage customer cars are blocking the car park, so you are told to park anywhere you can. Be careful to choose a spot which can't be blocked by a spectator or marshal – you'll look a right wally if you're late for the start!

20.30 hours. After parking the car, you take your club membership cards, RDS letter of insurance and documentation card to signing-on, inside the garage showroom. Take some paper and a pen as well; there could be some amendments on the Official Noticeboard you need to remember. Signing-on is laid out at a long table. You start at one end with your documentation card and have club membership cards checked, in addition to your entry form for any change of details. As you move along the table, your insurance letter is checked, you buy breakfast tickets, or lodge a team entry along with another crew, then finally you actually sign the RAC MSA form, which contains an indemnity clause, allowing you to officially start the rally. If Competition Licences are required, they will also be checked.

Your documentation card is signed and you are handed an envelope containing your time cards and rally plates (which should be placed on the car as described in the Regs). Ask what time you should come to collect your route and where it will be handed out. You are told to return to the showrooms at 22.15 hours.

21.00 hours. Back at the car, you have time to make everything ready for the start. The time cards are placed on the clipboard and you count 27 controls; that means 27 references to be plotted. This card can tell you a great deal about the format of the rally, so you should note that there are five sections timed to the second (TCs 6,9,12,15 and 19) and six Non-competitive sections, where time must not be made up (TCs 1,7,10,13,16 and MC2). There are also four unmarked boxes at the bottom, so expect some secret checks along the way.

A list of Black Spots hasn't been given out, so they will have to be plotted first once you have the route card, then there are bound to be Give Ways as well. That means you will be kept fairly busy for the 90 minutes between collecting your route and starting the rally. Make sure your belts are properly adjusted and your magnifier is at hand. Stow away your jacket. and case somewhere in the car where they won't move. Meanwhile, your driver should be cleaning the windscreen and lights, getting his side of things organized.

You will probably start chatting to the other crews, partaking in a bit of lighthearted ribbing, trying to gain the psychological edge! If you think the car directly behind could catch you, tell him you'll pull

Crews sign-on at the start, where rally officials check licences and amend entry forms. For road rallies, this documentation process usually takes place in a corner of the start garage where the Entries Secretary will be on duty. (*Large*)

out of his way as soon as possible – a show of consideration now will make up for the few seconds you will delay him during the rally.

22.00 hours. If your driver wanders away, tell him to be back at the car in time to help you plot the route. Walk round to the showroom about 10 minutes before you're due to collect the route as there may be last-minute amendments to take note of and the organizers may be generous enough to let you have your route card early.

As you hand over the documentation card containing a full set of signatures, a marshal will give out the route card. Check with him you have the right number of sheets (on the Holrus there was only one) and ask if there are any alterations.

Walk back to the car quickly, ignoring the delaying tactics of colleagues trying to coax you into a time-wasting chat. There are 32 Black Spots and Give Ways to be plotted along with the control references. You have about 85 minutes left, so there is no need to panic. Ask your driver to read out the Black Spots first (detailed as Out of bounds areas on the Holrus). It takes about 10 minutes to plot them.

The Give Ways are next and take about 20 minutes, so you still have plenty of time to plot the route. The organizers have shown the map changes and only one direction of departure is given – away from the start control. The first references detail 'via' points *en route* to TC1 (the first time control)

NEWTOWN & DISTRICT AUTOMOBILE CLUB LTD.

HOLRUS NOVICE RALLY 1983. Note. * Indicates controls timed to less than 1 minute.

<u>OUT OF BOUNDS AREAS</u>

200m RAD. OF 289 908½ MAP 137
KM SQ 06.96 Map 136
06.00 " "
07.00 " "
02.93 " "
16.92 " "
27.87 MAP 137
24.82 " "
25.82 " "

<u>GIVEWAYS.</u>

292895¾	088¼940½	196½906½
290895½	060¾935¼	175½851
268¾895¾	053961¾	188828½
248861¼	067½034	108¼938
242866	048½009½	162946
240½868½	101½047	
222¾824½	098987½	
146932½	186006½	
122¾949¾	161½952	

<u>ROUTE CARD.</u>

CONTROL	REFERENCE	APP	DEP	TIME	NOTES
START	136/119½919½		SW	10.45	Non competitive to TC1
VIA	118 913	W			
VIA	137/263 925	NW			
TC1	283 916	W		11.11	Care 292 903½
TC2	274 905½	ENE		11.19	
TC3	249 898	SW		11.28	
PCA	290 886½	N			
TC4	263½851	WSW		11.49	
PCB	242 866	SW			
TC5	225 838	E		12.08	
TC6*	136/185 831½	SE		12.17	Non competitive to TC7 very quiet to Anchor. P.R. Sensitive area.
TC7	180 861¼	SW		12.22	
TC8	196½906½	SE		12.29	
PCC	190 924¼	SSE			
TC9 *	167¼935¼	SE		12.40	Proceed quietly to Petrol at 179975 recover lost time at Petrol.
TC10	181008¼	E		12.53	
PCD	156½004½	SW			
TC11	133½001¼	NW		01.07	Care 138½999½
TC12 *	103½987	ESE		01.16	Non competitive to TC13 very quiet through Newmills and Manafon.
TC13	137¾032¼	SW		01.26	
TC14	101½047	E		01.34	
TC15*	067½034	SE		01.40	Non competitive to TC 16 Quiet and dipped headlights through Cefn Coch.
TC16	033 023½	ENE		01.44	
PCE	041¼014½	SW			
VIA	055½968	NE			
TC17	061940	N		02.06	
TC18	081¼947½	N		02.12	
PCF	110 949½	SSW			
VIA	130956¼	W			
TC19*	137 940	N		02.29	Non competitive to MC2 and damage in Bus Station car park, very quiet in Newtown.
MC2	107¼916	SE		02.37	

Max. lateness MC2 is 45 minutes.

Route card for the 1983 Holrus Novice Rally.

where the competitive motoring starts. Just as you start to plot the route, the first car pulls away from the start and this tends to heighten the tension inside your car, but ignoring it, you carry on plotting.

Some 45 minutes later, it's finished and you just have enough time to run across to a friend and quickly check your route with his. Back in the car, your driver has started the engine to warm it up and you strap yourself in, waiting to be called into line by one of the start area marshals. You notice that the glamorous beauty flagging away the Experts has long since disappeared to the warmth of the car showroom – it's a hard life being a Novice! As the car in front of you leaves the start, watch which way he turns. If no-one laughs, it must be the right way, so make sure you do the same; it does sound obvious, but you'd be surprised how many people get that wrong.

Have the time card resting on the door windowsill ready for the start control marshal to fill in the time and have a quick look at the clock, noting whether the organizers are using digital clocks (virtually foolproof) or conventional watches (which could produce reading errors).

The first section is the 'run out' and should be driven in a relaxed manner. Despite this, you should be reading the road to the driver, playing yourself into the event. You will undoubtedly find your driver will stop to adjust the car's lights again, this ritual seeming to be an incurable disease for drivers; no matter how many times they set the lights up, there is always room for improvement. If you catch up with

Time card for the 1983 Holrus Novice Rally.

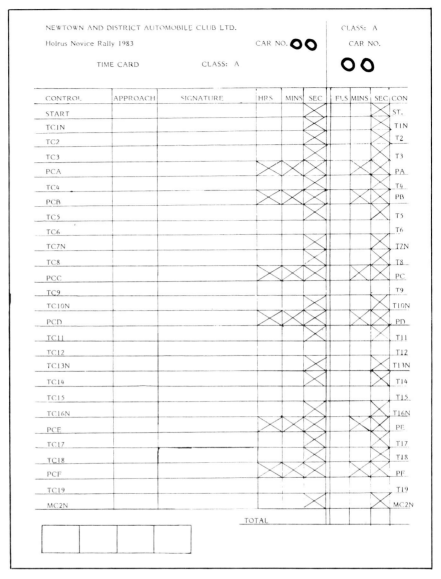

CONTROL	APPROACH	SIGNATURE	HRS	MINS	SEC	FLS	MINS	SEC	CON
START									ST.
TC1N									T1N
TC2									T2
TC3									T3
PCA									PA
TC4									T4
PCB									PB
TC5									T5
TC6									T6
TC7N									T7N
TC8									T8
PCC									PC
TC9									T9
TC10N									T10N
PCD									PD
TC11									T11
TC12									T12
TC13N									T13N
TC14									T14
TC15									T15
TC16N									T16N
PCE									PE
TC17									T17
TC18									T18
PCF									PF
TC19									T19
MC2N									MC2N
			TOTAL						

NEWTOWN AND DISTRICT AUTOMOBILE CLUB LTD.

Holrus Novice Rally 1983

TIME CARD CLASS: A CAR NO. OO

CLASS: A CAR NO.

CAR NO. OO

the car in front, don't overtake him unless you think he is going to be late as you will probably have to queue at the first control anyway. Keep reading the road, even though you are following him, and practise judging distances.

At the first control, see that the marshal fills in the correct time and wait for him to count you down. He will usually tell you 30 seconds, 15, 10, then 5-4-3-2-1-Go! When he shouts 15, your mouth will dry up! Whether it's your first or 101st rally, the same feeling of nerves is there. If it isn't then you may as well forget rallying as a sport and take up fishing!

Before you get the 'Go' you should be telling your driver what lies ahead. Count down from 5 out aloud along with the marshal. Some marshals like to hold onto the time card until they shout 'Go', but try and get it back a few seconds early so it can be safely stowed away before you shoot off down the road. Wind the window almost closed, leaving a small gap so you can hear the marshal, then wind it up completely once moving.

The Holrus is in December and it's freezing, so it's no real surprise to find you are soon running into patchy ice. In these conditions, your driver won't thank you for reading instructions late, particularly to warn of tight corners and T junctions! As you approach TC2, tell him which way to leave and what the road does. Wind down the window and have the time card ready for signing even before the car stops. Switch on the marshal light and tell your driver to dip his lights as soon as he sees the marshal – an

Some rallies add a bit of glamour to the start. Here Brian Cakebread and Jon Savage are flagged away by the lovely Miss Newtown and District AC. (*Speedsport*)

eyeful of powerful lamps will leave him dazzled and unable to see if you, in the approaching car, have the time card out of the window or are opening the door for him to lean inside. Only adopt the method of opening the door on a rainy night when the time card would otherwise get wet.

Unless you are given a time that is obviously wrong, don't waste time checking the clock at every control; wait until the final control in a competitive section before doing that, unless the marshal holds the clock in such a way that you can read it whilst he fills in the time card.

At TC6, the marshal will record your arrival time in hours, minutes and seconds. The next section is non-competitive and you are told to be especially quiet at the *Anchor Inn* – a PR-sensitive area. Tell your driver when he is approaching the area to drive very quietly. Your due time of arrival at TC7 is the hours and minutes that were recorded at TC6; the seconds can be forgotten about for now. There may be a queue at TC7, so when you arrive, find out what time the car in front is taking. If it's later than your time pull in front of him, but if he hasn't passed you in the previous section, recheck your required time!

As you arrive at the petrol halt, there are a number of cars waiting, their crews chatting and drinking coffee. You take on enough fuel for the remainder of the route and compare your total penalties with other navigators. There is a clock at the halt which shows the time on the watch at the next control (in

this case there is no 'In' or 'Out' control at the petrol halt). You should keep a close eye on the clock, bearing in mind the next control is about four miles away. You should also expect a long queue of competitors at that control, which could mean a fair degree of confusion, so spend as little time as necessary at the garage.

When checking the times of other crews, be prepared for a few shocks – there is always someone else better than you, but always be truthful about your own times. Navigators who give out wrong times soon have a bad reputation and find that times given to them in return soon begin to look suspect! But that doesn't mean to say you can't employ a little gamesmanship. 'Did you get that secret check?' is quite a good one to try, but don't be surprised if you get the reply: 'Yes. Both of them.' . . . *touché!*

When you arrive at the restart control for the second half there are about 15 cars queuing. The organizers on this particular event have told you to absorb all your MPL lateness at the petrol halt, so you are due to restart on the same Targa time you started the rally with. This is in fact contrary to the RAC MSA regulations, which state lateness should only be completely absorbed in a section of target less than four minutes or between an 'In' and 'Out' control at a rest halt. The organizers should have put two such controls at the petrol halt, but you were instructed to do so on the route card, so, 'yours is not to question why . . .'.

You should be careful at this point not to start automatically on the minute immediately after the car in front of you in the queue. There may have been some retirements already, meaning there should be gaps of several minutes between some cars. Always check first and on no account should you book into the control before the time you started the rally.

The second half passes much the same as the first and, before you know it, you are at the final control preceding the main control in Newtown. A feeling of achievement and total relaxation comes over you and the driver, but you should keep an eye on him in case he falls asleep! It may sound impossible, but even the best road rally driver can fall asleep at this point. You, the navigator, don't have such a problem, though; you have to make a copy of your penalties to check at the finish when the organizers post the provisional results.

Arriving back in Newtown for the final control, you then have your car checked for damage. There are penalties for damage to cars and also to property along the route. If you were to damage any property (a fence, for example) you should make a note of its location. There will be a damage declaration form to complete at the finish where you should either declare you have not caused damage, or if you have, to report the location. The organizers will then visit the property owner to make good the damage – sending the bill to you. If you do cause damage and fail to admit it, you risk losing your Competition Licence.

This rally finishes at a hotel in the centre of Newtown, so you are instructed to park in a nearby public car park. As you enter the finish hotel, a marshal waits to take your time card to the results team, and now it's time to join the scramble for breakfast. Rally crews are joined by marshals and hardy spectators who managed to last the distance to the finish. Drivers talk over close shaves and problems with their cars, while navigators chat about tricky sections of the route or the likely chances of getting further acquainted with a young lady marshalling a particular control.

By the time you have finished your breakfast, some results will have already been displayed. The Holrus used by far the best system. The time card had printed on it an extra column for the organizers' use. In this, the penalties at each control were entered and the strip was cut from the original card, then clipped to a 'washing line' strung across a wall. The strips were placed in position order, so that when a new result was posted, the others either side of it were simply slid along the line – they also used a colour coded system of time cards according to classes. You should check your times against those the organizers have declared, then check the arithmetic. If you notice an error, don't wait until the protest period to point it out, but write your query on a slip of paper and hand it to the results team for checking. You should also point out any errors you note in other crews' times, particularly the addition of their penalties – if the results team has added them up wrongly in favour of the crew, the other navigator is hardly going to shout about the mistake.

When all finishing cars' times have been displayed, the Clerk of the Course will issue a statement that results are provisional, along with the time the statement was made. Competitors then have 30 minutes in which to place an official written protest against other competitors, or indeed the organizers. Many a rally can be won by protesting, but it is a distasteful pastime and minor protests detract from the basic spirit of sport. Only if you have a severe grievance should you protest, and even then, there are those crews who refrain from doing so, knowing instead they are the moral victors anyway.

If there are no protests, the results will be pronounced 'final' and awards will be presented.

NEWTOWN AND DISTRICT AUTOMOBILE CLUB LTD.
HOLRUS NOVICE RALLY 1983.

DAMAGE DECLARATION FORM.
I hereby certify that ~~have~~ / have not CAUSED DAMAGE ON THE HOLRUS NOVICE RALLY.

Signed................. Car No. 55......

IF YOU HAVE CAUSED damage please give reference of damage...............
....
EXTENT OF DAMAGE...
....
....

The damage declaration form that had to be signed at the end of the 1983 Holrus.

No	Driver	Navigator	§	1	2	3	A	A	B	5	6	7	8	C	9	10	D	11	12	13	14	15	16	E	17	18	F	19	E	Penalties	Class
0	DERWYN EVANS	GUY WOODCOCK	A			R	E	T	I	R	E	D																		
1	PHILIP BENTLEY	N. HOULSTON	A			R	E	T	I	R	E	D																		
2	STEVE FLETCHER	CHRIS JONES	A			1			1.13				0.53			0.05							0.02		3.13	1st
3	JEFF TREMBLEY	GERAINT THOMAS	A	1			3	1.00		2.05			1.14		0.50			1		1.01		11.10	3rd
4	ANTONY HAYNES	PAUL JONES	A		2		2	1.07	1	2.28	1	1.14		0.52		1		NON FINISHER		
5	JOHN MORRIS	CHRIS FLAXELL	A			R	E	T	I	R	E	D																		
6	DEREK CROWTHER	ALUN EVANS	A		2		2	2	1.00		1.52		1	0.28		0.39				1.03		12.02	4th
7	JEFF ROGERS	ANTHONY JONES	A			R	E	T	I	R	E	D																		
8	PHIL ROACH	MICHAEL ROACH	A	1			2		1	1.16		1.59		1	0.15		0.22			1.59		10.51	2nd
9	MARK BLOCKTON	STEPHEN MARDO	A			R	E	T	I	R	E	D																		
10	"POLLY"	SARAH COLDWELL	A				2		1	1.32		5.51			0.54		0.43			1.28		13.28	6th
11	LES ROBERTS	JOHN FURNISS	A	1			5	3	0.00	1	2.00	1	1.06		1.10		1		3.54		20.10	8th
12	WYN LEWIS	HOWARD DAVIES	A				1		1	1.08		3.10			1.29		2.35			NON FINISHER		
13	KEITH BURGHAM	DAVID RICHARDS	A				1		1	0.29		2.12	3	0.47		0.24	11		2.21		22.13	11th
14	NIGEL HUGHES	MANDY JONES	A				1			0.16		1.17			0.27		0.04			9.35		12.39	5th
15	JOHN POWELL	DUNCAN ANNEGAR	A		1		3	1	0.08		2.39	1	1.26		1.13		1		7.46		20.18	9th
16	PLENTI RIGHTFOOT	IVOR STUTTER	A	1	2		4		7.03	2	2.16	2	1.50		2.02		2		4.00		30.11	12th
17	PETER AMMONDS	BRYAN THOMAS	A				3	2	1.14		2.32		1	0.35		1.03		1		4.26		16.50	7th
18	GORDON WRIGHT	ANDY OAKS	A			F	13	7	6.20	R	E	T	I	R	E	D														
19	WYN JENKINS	NEIL ASGERLEY	B	1			3	4	0.57	1	2.16	1	1.53		1.19		2		3.10		21.35	4th
20	S FARRINGTON	R MEREDITH	B	1	1		4	4	2.13	3	2.46	2	1.28		1.40	1		3.47		27.54	7th
21	MICK HUFFLER	BILL MORRIS	B	1	1		2	3	0.35	1	2.18	1	1.45		1.26	2	15	2.82		34.86	12th
22	PHILLIP EDWARDS	MIKE SIMPSON	B		1		2	2	0.50		2.23	4	1.19		0.31			2.22		16.25	1st
23	ALAN WATKINS	JOHN WHITTINGHAM	B		2		7	3	2.12	1	8.28	1	1.38		0.36		16	5.37		48.31	19th
24	MALCOLM ROCH	DAVID EDWARDS	B		1		2	3	2.08	F	20.52	1	1.01		0.44			3.29	1F 35.14	21st
25	RICHARD SOFF	JON CASHION	B		4		2	5	4.00	1	1.44	1	1.23		1.09			4.26		26.42	6th
26	PAUL WATTS	BRIAN TREVER	B				1	18	2	2.00		2.12		1	0.27		0.45			3.18		30.42	9th
27	J. BRUSTOCK	DAVE JONES	B			R	E	T	I	R	E	D																		
28	DAVID EVANS	BRIAN JONES	B	1	2		5	5	2.00		3.06	2	2.26	1	1.12		2		4.15		31.59	10th
29	JOHN ROLETTER	CHARLIE HULGARD	B				2	3	1.00		1.59	1	0.41		0.31			4.37		14.48	O/A WIN
30	IAN STEPHENS	BRIAN PHABSEY	B		2		4	1	1.48		2.26	1	1.10		1.15	1		4.59		20.38	2nd
31	CRAIG LOWE	ROBERT LYNCH	B	1	1		4	11	2.50	1	3.29	2	1.55		4.12	2		3.07		37.33	13th
32	DARREL WALKER	PHILLIP CLARKE	B	1	1		5	5	2.36	2	3.00	11	2.52	1	2.00	4	1	4.45		46.13	18th
33	STEPHEN PLUMMER	KEN GIBSON	B	1	1		5	6	3.30	1	4.00	3	2.06	1	2.06	3		6.32		39.14	14th

Rally results are often presented like this in their final form. Copies will be posted to every finisher after the rally.

Even though you may not have received an award, it is common courtesy to the organizers and the other competitors that you should attend, even though the attraction of getting home to a warm bed is probably foremost in your weary mind. You might be receiving an award yourself one day, and imagine how you would feel if only a handful of people were there to applaud.

Before you leave the hotel to go home, find the Clerk of the Course and ask him to sign your Competition Licence if you need it upgrading. He may do it on the spot, or take your licence from you and return it by post during the following week. At the same time, take the opportunity of thanking him for organizing such a good rally – their's is sometimes a thankless task and the thought will be appreciated.

The drive home will seem endless, but your driver should at least have had the chance for a nap at the finish whilst you have been checking results. If, however, you notice him nodding off behind the wheel, tell him to stop for you to take over. If the thought of your driving terrifies him, it will probably wake him up enough to carry on driving, but failing that, park up for half an hour and sleep. A brisk walk up and down the road before starting again should do the trick or have something cold to drink. When you do arrive back at home, you may find you have gone past the point of wanting to sleep immediately, so use the time to go over the route again on the map, marking any tricky junctions and bends for future reference. You should make a habit of doing this after every event, aiming to build up a comprehensive set of map markings, which can be transferred to a new map in due course.

All that remains is to check the results when a printed set arrives in the post the following week. Study them together with the route, possibly going over them with your driver, so you can pinpoint any areas which need improvement. It does no harm to start a graph of finishing positions – all this information will prove invaluable when searching for a sponsor.

5

Advanced Navigating

Basic navigating techniques are easy to grasp; even a few drivers have been known to pick up a map now and again without getting lost! Completing a rally is rewarding, but the next step is to start winning rallies regularly. It is a case of gaining experience, as in any other sport; however, the knowledge of how to use that experience is the key which will unlock the secret of success.

The will to win is an essential part of success in rallying: it is that undefinable quality that enables you to push yourself almost beyond your limit. Road rallying tests your limitations very quickly. You are expected to stay awake all night long; to be able to make split-second decisions (correct ones at that); and to be able to convey your own enthusiasm and vitality to your driver when he starts flagging.

On night rallies, the danger time is between the hours of 3 and 4 o'clock in the morning. The human body is then at its lowest ebb and, if the rally organizer is worth his salt, that is the time he will throw in some trickery to catch out the unwary. Before progressing in the sport you must sit down and ask yourself whether you are committed enough to continue; whether you have the will to win – nobody can teach you that, it's entirely up to you.

What *can* be learned are some of the tricks of the trade that current navigators use to their advantage and which a good organizer should be on his guard against. Couple to these tricks a comprehensive collection of maps marked with extra useful information and you are armed with the most powerful weapons in the sport, but you must have the confidence to use them.

Map marking
One of the secrets of success lies in your maps. They will eventually contain information gathered by your own experiences or gleaned from others (by fair

means or foul!). You will learn the best system of map marking which suits you as you progress. There are standard methods which are universally accepted and they are fine to use as a guideline, but it is far better to adopt your own unique method as quickly as possible.

Map markings contain the basic information which will allow you to complete the rally with the minimum of drama, and that in itself will ease tension that can so easily ruin a crew's performance. They will include junctions which are particularly difficult to find, corners which are dangerous or tricky, and sections of the map notorious for being inaccurately portrayed in print. These latter points are not to be blamed on the excellent job carried out by Ordnance Survey, but there is a physical limit to how much information can be depicted on a map. If there are a number of very sharp corners (hairpins for example) occurring within, say, 200 metres, it is impossible to show them on a 1:50 000 map, for the simple reason that the roads are shown on the map by a line disproportionately thick – a typical yellow road is shown to have a width of about 100 metres. Bearing that in mind, the maps are amazingly accurate and by far the best of any produced worldwide (with the possible exception of Finland).

There are OS maps available which are even more accurate, such as the 1:25 000 Outdoor Leisure maps. However, their production is limited to areas of the country which are popular with hikers. A similar scale of map is also produced, but for the average rally, the cost of covering the entire route would be astronomical and according to the RAC rules 1:50 000 scale maps are the only ones used to officially define rally routes.

Markings giving information on bad corners, dangerous sections and tricky junctions should be marked boldly – a draughtsman's drawing pen is

Oops! Now this calls for a map marking. Every mark has usually cost someone some bodywork damage. Ron Douglas is the unfortunate victim here; he is running back up the road with a warning triangle, leaving the poor navigator to sort himself out. (*Davies*)

best to give a small accurate marking in black ink, or marks in ballpoint pen are adequate. Make sure you always write in waterproof ink as maps tend to get wet on a rainy night and markings smudge infuriatingly quickly! All other markings should be made with waterproof felt tip pen, in either red, yellow or green – colours which appear translucent and don't completely obliterate the map underneath.

Your first marking of a map should be to transfer the grid line numbers to the body of the map. The latest Second Series maps already show these, the grid line numbers being repeated across the map at 10km intervals. However, they are printed in light blue and can take some finding in moments of panic. It is a good idea to mark over them with a red felt tip pen. You should also mark the numbers of the adjoining sheets around the perimeter of the map so you know which map to switch to in a hurry when the route moves from one map to another. If the route zigzags between two maps, you could always sketch the roads from the other in the margin of the one you are using, but it's only advisable to do this for short distances.

Experience will tell you when it can be expected for rallies to use constant changes of adjoining maps: you should then start joining your own maps together. Buy a spare sheet of one map and cut a strip five kilometres deep from the edge which joins the other map. Carefully trim off the margin (for future use) and glue the overlap to correspond with the correct grid lines on the other map. You now have an overlap which avoids the irritating changes of map every few miles or so. The margin which was stripped from the cut map should now be glued to the extension strip to provide both a reference to grid line numbers and a protective border. If you are using maps with overlaps, remember not to fall into the trap of forgetting to duplicate Black Spots and other route information on the added portion.

Markings on the body of the map should be compact, but not too small as to make them unreadable. The information which needs to be conveyed will change as you progress through the sport. Starting off with not-as-map junctions and corners is sufficient, aiming to progress on to marking brows or crests in the road which could be straight, or have a corner directly after them. A line drawn through the road with the letter 'B' or 'C' to indicate the position of a brow is the best method.

Dangerous corners should be marked with 'caution' boards on the rally itself, but sometimes they disappear. Marking them on your map with exclamation marks is a good method and they can be graded by using two or perhaps three marks. When copying markings from other navigators' maps, it is important you ask exactly what each mark indicates. Cattle grids and gates are best marked by a line across the road and either 'grid' or 'gate' written alongside. Gates on the blind side of a crest in the road are best cautioned as well – they may be closed!

Featureless moorland roads are a navigating nightmare. If the occasion arises to drive over popular moorland stretches, it is a good idea to mark down all landmarks, remembering that a little hump in the road which you can see over during the day can turn into a blind brow when using driving lights at night. Marking which junctions are signposted can save valuable seconds on a rally, allowing your driver to pick out the junction position well in advance. In fact any information regarding junction spotting will prove invaluable. You should also note whether junctions feature a grass triangle and whether a particularly tight hairpin junction can be cut short by driving across the banking. The same applies to roads through farmyards, when quite often it's possible to take a short cut. There was one particularly well-known such short cut in the middle of the old one-inch map 128 – through a gate into a farmyard, then immediately right, down a bank and back on to the exit road. It cut out about a quarter of a mile, that is until, on one rally, the top crews discovered to their cars' cost that the farmer had excavated foundations for a garage at the bottom of the bank!

If a short cut is impossible and the hairpin in question is impossible to negotiate in one manoeuvre (even by a handbrake turn), then look to the idea of either turning your car around before the junction and approaching it in reverse, or driving past it to a handy farm entrance where you can turn the car around. If there are two 'impossible' hairpins within 200 metres, it may be worthwhile travelling in reverse for the distance between them.

Fords are another useful marking worth exploration. Again, experience of certain areas will bring knowledge of water crossings used. There is generally a right and a wrong way to drive through them. Rarely should fords be charged at like a bull. Time spent carefully picking a way through will pay dividends and you may find the water shallower either slightly upstream, or downstream, from the obvious way across. There is also the case (although not advisable for safety reasons) of a particularly enterprising crew who found they could drive their small car across a footbridge alongside the ford – much to the surprise of the spectators standing on the bridge at the time!

Many of the lowest-grade roads shown on a map (white roads) are usable, some even being tarmaced. The customary way of marking these 'goers', as they are known, is to colour them in with a felt-tip pen – yellow or green are the most popular colours. Those which you are unsure of are best left unmarked, but those which are impossible to use should be marked with a black cross. Some 'whites' are only drivable in one direction – generally downhill! These should be clearly marked 'down only', but some could be passable uphill in dry weather; further investigation may be necessary. Write a letter 'R' alongside rough 'whites'. These roads could play havoc with a low-slung exhaust system or could take longer to drive down than a slightly longer yellow road alternative.

Whilst competing on a rally, always have a pencil close at hand so you can mark information on the map. Just a line through the road will be enough to jog your memory when you have the time to think about it. By far the best method of collecting markings is by investigation yourself, but sometimes when contesting a nationwide championship this will be impractical. For this reason, many enterprising navigators advertise markings for sale, usually reasonably priced, and they are ideal as a starting point, especially as an indication of white road 'goers'. You may also find yourself being introduced to a new, better method of marking certain information on the map. Time and money spent on amassing this information before a rally is completely justified, for during a rally, every marking gained has invariably been at the cost of an expensive car body modification or a lost exhaust system.

Tricks of the trade

Thorough knowledge of a subject always gives you an advantage, but it is left to the individual to exploit that advantage. Learning these tricks of the trade comes with experience, and using them allows a navigator to manipulate rules without breaking them. It is a form of gamesmanship exercised with rally organizers, but it should never involve the flagrant breaking of rules, nor any unsporting behaviour.

Even before the rally, it is possible to gather information, starting with the Regs. Read the organizers' Foreword; it could give something away about the route. Look through the list of acknowledgements – garage owners are usually named and it is often possible to find the halfway

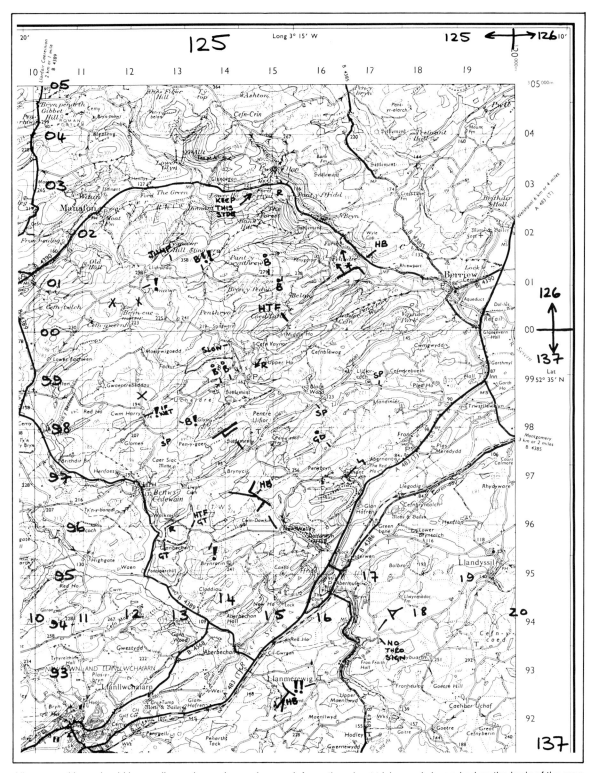

All map markings should be small, concise and conspicuous. Information about tricky roads is marked on the body of the map, with adjoining map numbers marked around the border. Extra grid line numbers have also been added to ease plotting.
(*Crown copyright*)

GT	gate
GD	cattle grid
B	crest or brow
R	rough
! - !!	caution
HB	handbrake hairpin
HTF	hard to find junction
o	flat out i.e. **B̊**
SP	signpost
⌐	unmarked kink
↙	one way only (usually downhill)
✕	no goer

petrol halt garage mentioned inadvertently. The Police authorities are named and thanked; this, too, gives a clue about which areas the route passes through. Try talking to the Clerk of the Course and ask him which areas he is using. If the rally is in an area strange to you, tell him you need to mark your new maps and that you don't want to waste your time marking up a complete map if only a small part is being used. Ask him if the route is going to be rough and how many petrol halts there will be. Also ask him, in confidence, for his accurate mileages to each petrol halt, so you don't overload the car with unnecessary extra fuel.

He may choose to leave some of your questions unanswered, but if you keep them relevant, yet not too obvious, he will most likely give the answers. You should be aiming to arrive at the rally start with a fairly shrewd idea of the route, and if time permits, you should have explored the area beforehand – but refrain from out-and-out practising. The passage of a rally will undoubtedly be accepted (and enjoyed) by householders along the route, provided it is on the Saturday night in question. Private rallies just before the weekend will soon alienate them.

There are many ways of gleaning information about the route of the event you are about to enter. The RAC MSA imposes a six-week gap on the use of the same road, so if there has been another rally in that area within six weeks, try and lay your hands on a copy of that rally route – the same roads cannot possibly be used. That should account for a certain area of the maps. For the rest, get hold of a copy of previous routes for your intended rally as clubs tend to be parochial. If the roads used previously don't digress into unusable areas, put your money on them being used again. Read the reports of last year's rally from *Motoring News*, *Autosport* and *Rally Sport.*

If you do choose to have a quiet look around on the morning or afternoon of the rally, plan to have lunch at a country pub and ask the locals where they think the route will be going. Prior knowledge of the route in this way is fair game. Think as the rally organizer would and you should be able to piece together a good educated guess at the route.

You should mark down the unexpected: patches of mud, gravel on junctions, hard-to-find junctions and in some cases even short-term hazards such as deep puddles of water in the road, farm machinery parked on the road and farm dogs running free! In a winter rally, water running across the road could turn to sheet ice by the early hours of the morning, whilst a patch of mud on a summer rally would soon turn to dust, creating fog when churned up by car wheels. If you are certain a stretch of moorland road is being used, there is nothing to stop you making rough pacenotes for the section instead of using your map – although these will generally be safety notes rather than pure pacenotes.

When you arrive at the start of the rally, your first obstacle is the car's noise check. There are various standards of noise check, and rally cars are usually prepared to a high degree which produces little noise anyway, but 'rules is rules!'. Check the noise readings of cars before you in the queue and make sure you are happy with the check location. Close all car windows during the check, and if your car fails, ask for the car to be turned around to be checked from the other direction – particularly if your car's exhaust pipe points towards the noise meter. Keep a record of noise readings from previous rallies and if all else fails show it to the noise official to convince him his meter is faulty in some way.

Before you receive your rally route, chat to the other crews and gain the psychological advantage. Never appear nervous or unsure, and when you have collected your route card *never* run back to your car – that's a sure sign of weakness. If possible, plot the route away from the car. Find a well lit and quiet place – a hotel room if you are wealthy enough, or a spare office at the start garage (with the owner's permission, of course). When finished, find the rival navigator you respect the most and check your route with his. This happens to such an extent on top-flight championship rallies that the leading crews all agree to follow the same route – even if it is wrong!

However, if you think you have found a short cut that nobody else knows of, don't mark it on the map until after you have checked the 'proper' route with the other navigators – don't be surprised if at the finish you discover they all took the short cut – devious bunch that they are. Also, look carefully at the route for possible double usage of a road – it is only against rally rules for organizers to use the same road twice, but be very careful about using the road against rally traffic. Find out if the organizers are recording the number order of cars arriving at each passage control (they could do so by equipping each control with a clock and instructing the marshal to record the rough passage time on his check sheet). If no record is being kept, an advantage can be gained from the organizers' inefficiency. It may be possible to deliberately bypass a passage control, visiting it later to collect a signature during a non-competitive section when you have enough time to spare.

There may be lower penalties for missing out a passage control than for missing a time control. If the rally timing is poor and you find yourself about to run into Maximum Permitted Lateness, you will have to cut out a section of route and leapfrog ahead to stay within 'fail time'. You should always bear this in mind when plotting the route, looking for a handy loop section which could be cut. Rallies have been won on this method, so even the top navigators should beware. The system of timing rallies is such that if you fail to visit a control (which includes visiting it outside your MPL), you are due at the following control at your original due time, which means you will collect an extra time penalty. The ideal situation is therefore one where you cut the minimum number of controls and arrive at the subsequent one on your original start time (with the Targa system, that's your car number).

After your route has been plotted and your brain is throbbing from the intake of all this information, you should seek out the official photographer and press reporters. Make friends with them (a pint is generally the quickest way with the press!), so they will remember to send your picture to the relevant papers and the reporter will know who to write about.

During the run out to the first control, start reading the map to your driver so you are both familiar with each other if it is your first rally together, or to refresh memories if you are an established crew. Note how early you arrive at the first control; it will give some indication of how much time the organizer has 'pruned' from his route and how much time you consequently can expect to drop. Adopt a slick control procedure to remain stationary for as little time as possible and always tell your driver which way to depart before you deal with the marshal. In return, your driver can be expected to inform you of the presence of young ladies marshalling the control in the time honoured fashion by shouting 'crumpet!' – he will see them first, as you will have your head down looking at the map. Always have a spare pen at the ready, particularly if you are running as the first car on the road, because marshals always seem to misplace theirs at the last minute. But always insist that they continue to use that same pen for everyone else – if your time card has a time entered in black and the rest of the field has times written in the blue Biro which the marshal found after you left his control, a finger of accusation will be pointing at you at the finish.

At some point in the rally you will come across either a slower car or a quicker one. If the following car is obviously much faster than you, pull over and let him through. The same should apply if you catch a slower car. If, however, the slower car is not driven by a gentleman, there are several ways of dealing with him. Following with your auxiliary lights on may defeat him, or try 'pushing' him into overshooting a junction. If all else fails, you will eventually arrive at a control and it's there you can overtake. You should drive past him and stop in such a position that he cannot repass you. Then, in your best shouting voice, gain the marshal's attention and try to have your time card filled in before the other crew's. If you succeed, you will gain roughly a 10-second advantage in leaving the control, and because you are the quicker crew, that advantage should be increased.

The following car of a pair, though, generally has the advantage. Once within sight of the front car, the crew of the following one will have advance warning of corners and particularly junctions, closing the distance extremely rapidly. If both crews are evenly matched, it is obviously to the leader's advantage to lose his tail. There is the time taken at controls to benefit from, then you can tell your driver to lightly touch the brake pedal more often than necessary, so the following driver will think you are braking for corners which don't really exist. If it is a dry night, driving in the dust at the roadside will create a fog behind you, slowing the other car, but if you have a short cut approaching, it will be in your favour to let the other car pass before you get to it. It's then you will find he knows it as well and the tables are turned!

In rallying territory strange to you, be on the lookout for spectators in odd places – they are there for a reason and that reason is probably to see you make a mistake. You should also be ready for controls which are slightly off-plot. Their change in position could open an opportunity for a short cut. Say, for example, they are 200 metres before the junction at which you expected to find them, you might be able to take the 'wrong' road away from the junction to your advantage.

The situation may occur when another competitor informs you of a route blockage and suggests you make the same detour as he does. In a word – don't. If for some reason the route is blocked, that section naturally becomes impassable and will be scrubbed, but you should investigate the blockage. This may only be a temporary blockage, in which case you can continue unhindered along the route. You may then meet the detouring crews at a control which they have had to approach from the wrong direction in order to regain the rally route – in such a case you should insist they are all given a penalty for that infringement. If you meet them at any other point, you will be safe in the assumption that their detour has cost them time penalties. When a route blockage is permanent, there will be enough other crews queued up to add their weight to an argument for having that section cancelled. Never under any circumstances take another crew's word for a route change – the only route amendment to be heeded is one given to you in writing by the organizers, which you will be expected to sign for as proof of receipt.

Booking in early at a control rarely happens with a Targa timing system, but it can happen when organizers mix timing methods during the rally. For organizational purposes, it may suit the Clerk of the Course to run a Targa system for ordinary timed-to-the-minute sections, but to use a separate system for timed-to-the-second Selective sections. Selectives maybe run to BBC Time (proper time of day), in which case your route card will show the due arrival time of the first car – make sure you don't book in early. Similarly, at the Selective finish, it is not uncommon for crews to 'clean' the section and beat the target time the organizers have set. This beating the target will not involve penalties because you will be making up time under the three-quarter ruling, except in one case, namely when you start the section on your original due time (*i.e.* the time you started the rally with). Without realizing it, you may book into a Selective finish before you are legally allowed to. So, be extremely aware of this if you start a Selective back on your original rally start time – if you *do* arrive early, of course, you should wait for your correct time.

At the rally finish, you will have a shrewd idea if any protests are going to be made. You should be aware of all protests. They may not involve you directly, but a crew placed lower than you may move ahead. You may also be asked to give evidence at any meeting of the Stewards, in which case you are obliged to attend and should deal only in facts, always looking at situations objectively.

6

Co-driving

In special stage rallying, the occupier of the 'Hot Seat' undergoes a name change. These co-drivers, as opposed to navigators, have long been the proverbial 'sacks of spuds', simply there to satisfy the rules and regulations while the driver hurls his car headlong at the scenery in forests. He has been unable to assist the driver, yet his job is just as demanding, and it requires even more skills than are needed from his road rallying counterpart. Many of the sport's top co-drivers started rallying life as road rally navigators, where they learned a sixth sense for timing and the ability to make a split-second decision in the heat of the moment. Navigators are able to look at two points on a map and accurately estimate the travelling time. Many co-drivers have never tackled a road rally, but few of these have had the ability of exploiting their skills to the full.

Almost every World Championship team has a British co-driver actively involved, whether as a competitor or in team management. At the time of writing, active co-drivers listed included the names of Terry Harryman, Fred Gallagher, Ian Grindrod, Mike Broad, Rob Arthur, Dave Whittock, Ronan Morgan, Phil Short, Neil Wilson, John Spiller and Kevin Gormley amongst many others. Other famous co-drivers have progressed into management and organization: Henry Liddon, Stuart Turner, Jim Porter, John Davenport, John Brown and the first ever World Champion Co-driver, Dave Richards are examples. All have a common link – they all started as road rally navigators.

A co-driver has to be more of an office manager than does a navigator. Special stage rallying brings a new dimension to the sport with the inclusion of a service crew in the team – the co-driver is the one who habitually has the task of managing them, too. A successful co-driver must be decisive and have a feel for general organization, the more meticulous the better. But he must also possess the indefinable quality of being able to lift his driver from the deepest depression and relieve him of pressure. In short, a co-driver must be a human computer, ready to give the correct answer to any question, anytime.

SPECIAL STAGE RALLIES

The competitive portions of special stage rallies always take place on private land. These stages are joined by link (or road) sections, familiarly on public roads. They regularly start and finish at the same place and are held in daylight. Service areas are included, where the team mechanics repair or modify the competing cars and change wheels and tyres, much like a racing team with its pit stops.

Cars are modified to a much greater extent, with a need for more basic equipment than a road rally car. Regulations require cars to include more safety equipment, such as roll-cages fitted inside the cars, full-harness seat belts, fireproof bulkheads front and rear in the passenger compartment, laminated glass windscreens and fire extinguishers. The crew must also wear approved crash helmets and are not allowed to smoke on the special stages.

The sport of special stage rallying is ordinarily more professional than its public road parent. There is a much greater range of events, extending into National, International and Open International status. At the lower end of the spectrum, individual clubs promote single-venue rallies in a compact area entirely within the confines of private land. Complete championships have been organized around this type of event. Further up the ladder come Restricted-status multi-venue rallies, National-status championship rallies and fully fledged Internationals held over several days (and nights). In Great Britain, we have the complete range, culminating in the ultimate: a rally included

Ian Grindrod sits with Jimmy McRae waiting to start a stage on the Manx International. Ian is one of an elitist band who have successfully made the grade from road rallying into World Championship events. (*Large*)

in the World Championship – the RAC Rally of Great Britain.

Types of special stage

Special stages vary with the level of competition. At the lower end of the range come tests over farm tracks and disused airfields. Military land provides rough stages at venues like Salisbury Plain, or smooth, fast tarmac at Eppynt in Wales and Otterburn on the Scottish border. The laws of Ireland, the Isle of Man and Jersey offer the opportunity of special stage rallying over everyday roads specially closed to the public. But by far the most widely used are the tracks built and maintained by the Forestry Commission, which offer superb gravel road special stages. These stages have to be paid for, however, and there is a restriction on their usage. The RAC MSA governs the allocation of these forests to motor clubs and appoints Forestry Liaison Officers as the link between the Forestry Commission and the clubs concerned.

The vast majority of special stages have routes kept secret from competitors – with severe penalties imposed by the RAC if anyone is found to be reconnoitring them. Some organizers, however – particularly those of tarmac stage rallies – do allow competitors to travel over them beforehand to familiarize themselves with the roads and possibly make notes (known as pacenotes) to help them during the actual event. Most continental rallies allow pacenoting, but take it a step further and allow high-speed practising as well. All special stages are

At club level, scrutineering is basically the same as for road rallies. Here, whilst the Scrutineer checks the car's lights and indicators, the driver has already put the helmets on the roof ready for inspection. The co-driver stands by, just to keep and eye on the Scrutineer! (*Large*)

closed to the public, so there is no danger of anyone coming the other way.

Grades of special stage rally
The grading of special stage rallies by status is similar to that for road rallying, but far higher grades are reached.

Single venue. These are the lowest grade as a rule. If they are Closed (C) status, a Competition Licence is not required, but membership of the organizing club is necessary. They frequently feature a disused airfield, a racing circuit, or a complex of roads in safari parks, although they can centre on a forest complex. As a starting point, they provide cheap events and are ideal for gaining experience. A number of championships have sprung up stringing these rallies together on a regional basis and are fiercely contested.

Restricted multi-venue (R). A Restricted-grade Competition Licence is needed to enter these events in addition to membership of an invited club. Association championships are comprised of these rallies and the stages can vary from basic farm track tests to forest stages.

National (N). With the odd exception, these form the qualifying rounds of a major championship. A British National-grade licence is needed by competitors. Stages are typically of high quality, using forests that often feature in the more important Internationals, or use tarmac stages of similar quality. Individual stages are normally longer than in lower-grade events, and there may be fewer chances of repairing a damaged car owing to stricter servicing rules. The crews and cars are expected to be of a higher standard.

International (I). These are the rallies which can be entered by anyone holding an International-grade licence – whether British or foreign. They are not only governed by the RAC General Competition Regulations (Blue Book), but also have to comply with the Sporting Code of the Federation International du Sport Automobile (FISA) based in Paris – the overall governing body of motor sport worldwide – whose regulations are published annually in what is coloquially known as the Yellow Book. These Internationals can span any number of days and have any length of route, and they qualify for inclusion in FISA-recognized championships, culminating in the World Championship.

Officials

The family tree of special stage officials is similar to that for road rallying. The Clerk of the Course, Secretary of the Meeting and Chief Marshal remain, although their importance is magnified. Complementing this nucleus are several additional officials. Stage Commanders are appointed to take charge of each particular stage, acting as a mini-Clerk of the Course. Doctors are necessary to satisfy RAC safety rules. A Timekeeper is required, and familiarly an Equipment Officer is appointed to handle the specialized equipment and distribute it where necessary. Rescue and recovery vehicles may also be employed to clear a blockage on a stage after an accident or breakdown. A radio network is often used so that various officials can be in touch with incidents at all times, and someone will be given the task of controlling spectators.

As events increase in status, new officials appear. A Press Officer handles publicity and information, whilst a Competitor Liaison Officer helps to clear any misunderstandings between crews and officials. Progressing into International events, key officials will have to be recognized by the RAC MSA, which grades and licenses Scrutineers and Timekeepers. RAC Observers will need to be appointed and an RAC Steward will have to be present. FISA events will need FISA Stewards and Observers from foreign countries (and their expenses have to be met by the organizing club!). On International rallies, it is not uncommon to have upwards of 30 key officials on duty – it all seems never-ending.

Types of control

Main controls, time controls and passage controls are used in much the same way as in road rallying. In addition there are Special Stage Start and Special Stage Finish controls – time controls preceding stage starts are ordinarily called Stage Arrival controls. The penalties for arriving early, late or not visiting these controls vary from road rallying.

Main controls are sited at the start and finish of the rally and are familiarly suffixed 'In' or 'Out'.

A marshal counts this Sunbeam down from the stage start clock as his lovely assistant makes a note of the exact time the car starts the test. Behind her is the control board used to depict a special stage start. (*Large*)

As the car crosses the stage flying finish line, a marshal uses a flag to signal to the stage finish marshals to freeze the clock. Where there is no direct line of sight between the flying finish and the Stop control, a bell or buzzer is used instead of the flag. (*Large*)

They also appear before and after a rest halt. Time controls may appear before and after a service area to make sure competitors are restricted timewise to the extent of repairs they can carry out on a damaged car. Passage controls are typically used as time card collection points, where information of a crew's performance is fed back to a results team, allowing interim results to be produced.

The order of controls is habitually Stage Arrival (which ends a road section), Stage Start (where cars start at minute intervals, or in special cases at 30-second intervals), Stage Flying Finish (end of competitive driving) and Stage Finish (where crews stop to receive a stage time).

Timing

Unlike road rallies, special stage event timing bears a direct relationship to the correct time of day. Although there are several recognized methods of timing stage events, Target timing is the most widely used. It is a seemingly foolproof method where each individual section, whether stage or link, has a set time in which it is to be completed. A period of penalty-free lateness is generally allowed, to deter crews from driving too fast on public roads – and there are penalties for booking into controls early. Once the penalty-free period has been consumed, time penalties in the order of 10 seconds per minute late are awarded, but some rallies exclude competitors once their penalty-free lateness has been consumed.

At the rally start you will be given a set of time cards, probably with instructions about where each card will be collected by a marshal. You will be notified of your start time, and to this you add the target time for the first road section. That is your due arrival time at the following control – and so it goes on. Booking in at a main control (Out) ordinarily carries a penalty of a minute per minute late or early.

The organizers will advise you of the maximum penalty-free lateness period (if any!) and of what penalties you will receive after that time – the most common penalty is exclusion. This lateness period is measured between consecutive main controls and is cumulative, just as in road rally Targa timing. Time lost can never be recovered, but your accumulated penalty-free lateness returns to zero after visiting each main control – providing, of course, you book out on time.

Special stages have their own timing method. Timing to the previous whole minute is used for link or road sections, whilst stages are timed-to-the-second. A bogey time is established for the stage, based on a 60mph average for gravel or loose surfaces, and 70mph for wholly sealed (asphalt or concrete) surfaces. A target time is also set for the stage, familiarly at something like a 30mph average. Beating the bogey time will achieve nothing except boosting a driver's ego – you will be allocated the bogey time as a penalty. By recording a time for the stage between bogey time and target time, your penalties will be the actual time taken. Exceeding the target time will give you penalties of your actual time taken, plus the time over target going towards your cumulative road time lateness.

For the purpose of target timing, the period between a stage arrival control and a stage start control is 'dead' time. You may find there has been a delay in opening the stage for some reason and a queue of cars builds up. No penalty is given because of this dead time. When you book into the arrival control, the marshal there may allot you a stage start time – unusually three minutes ahead. If, for any reason, you are unable to start the stage at that specified time due to a fault of the organizers, you will be given a fresh start time by the stage start marshal, who should also initial the alteration. If no stage start time is given by the arrival control marshal, you will be expected to start the stage on the next available minute, which is given to you by the start marshal – by then, of course, you should be

wearing your helmet and have your seat belts fastened. If you fail to start at your allotted time – tough luck, the clock still ticks away.

At the stage finish, you will be given your time in hours, minutes and seconds. If there is no time control for stage departure, your starting time for the following road section will be your stage finish time less the seconds, *i.e.* only the time in hours and minutes. By adding the target time for the next section, you arrive at the due time for booking into the following control.

Just like road rallying, if you arrive early, you can wait for your due time without penalty – unless either the ASRs state otherwise, or it is an FISA-governed event. Rules for Internationals do vary from normal club rallies and are dealt with in a later chapter.

Route definition

The rally route is given to co-drivers on a route card, or in a road book. The method of defining the route by Tulip diagrams is now virtually universal in its acceptance, although some events still use six-figure map references. As in road rallying, the route has to be checked with the RAC Route Authorization Department, and householders along the intended route must be visited, but generally the rules are slackened for daylight stage rallies. The official map is still the 1:50 000 OS; however, the actual route of a special stage on a 'secret' rally is not allowed to be marked on the map. Nor can hazards within stages be marked on the map, as this is viewed as having pace notes. At one time, maps were banned on stage

A typical stage finish clock. With its LCD display, it is easily read, even in direct sunlight. The button on the right is to freeze the time at which a car passes the flying finish line. (*Large*)

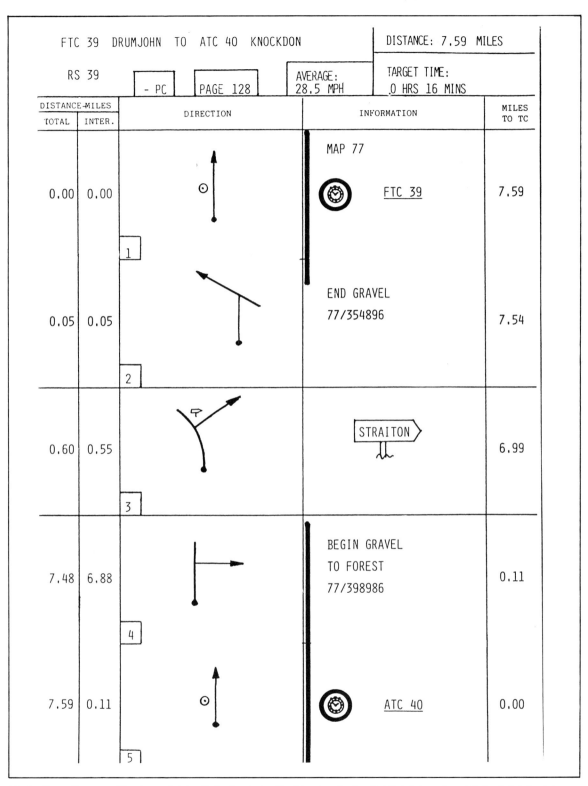

FTC 39 DRUMJOHN TO ATC 40 KNOCKDON				DISTANCE: 7.59 MILES	
RS 39	- PC	PAGE 128	AVERAGE: 28.5 MPH	TARGET TIME: .0 HRS 16 MINS	

DISTANCE-MILES		DIRECTION	INFORMATION	MILES TO TC
TOTAL	INTER.			
0.00	0.00		MAP 77 ⊚ FTC 39	7.59
0.05	0.05	[1]	END GRAVEL 77/354896	7.54
0.60	0.55	[2]	STRAITON	6.99
7.48	6.88	[3]	BEGIN GRAVEL TO FOREST 77/398986	0.11
7.59	0.11	[4]	⊚ ATC 40	0.00
		[5]		

Most rallies will use road books containing Tulip diagrams, like this page from a Scottish International Rally. It details distances in totals, intervals and countdown to the next control.

After the flying finish, cars are slowed down and crews collect their time from the Stop control marshals. If you overshoot this control, you should never reverse back to it – the co-driver should get out and walk back to have his time card filled in. (*Large*)

events (other than on the RAC Rally). After a massive lobbying campaign by the country's top co-drivers, the RAC MSA changed its ruling, but only allows the points where a stage enters and exits a forest to be marked down.

Unlike road rallies, the route is handed out as soon as the crew has completed documentation. The road book contains all the information necessary for a crew to complete the rally. It will be fairly thick, containing somewhere between eight and 12 instructions per page. At the front of the road book will be additional route instructions, and usually there is a list of six-figure references of all controls as well, but Black Spots are rarely listed. There could also be a list of 'standard' times indicating the arrival of car number 1, but it will be pointed out if any time shown is an official stage opening time. Tulip diagrams of the stages could also be included in the road book, or could be handed to competitors as they start the stage.

The road book pages are headed with the section number and target time, sometimes with the total section distance and average speed as well. Against each Tulip diagram instruction will be a total distance figure, showing how far you are from the previous control. An intermediate distance may also be shown, which is the distance from the previous instruction. These distances should have been measured by the organizers driving the route in a car fitted with an accurate tripmeter – organizers usually inform competitors of the distance between two specific landmarks, so crews can check this distance against their own tripmeter reading and make the necessary adjustments so they coincide. There is usually also a space on the page for additional written instructions, such as areas of extreme quiet, road names and numbers, and signposted (SP) destinations.

Equipment

A few specialized bits and pieces need to be added to the basic list of equipment for navigators, since co-drivers must be able to measure both time and distance accurately. The usual pens and pencils,

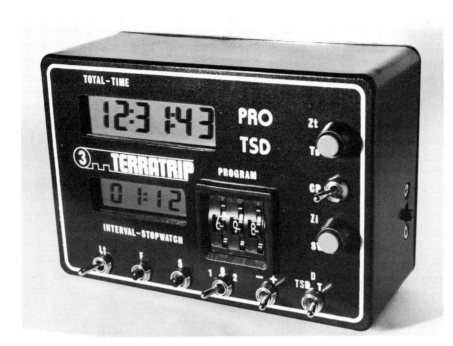

romer and clipboard are still kept, but more expensive items are needed.

Tripmeter. This device accurately measures distances travelled and will need to be zeroed at various points along the rally route. The choice of tripmeter is unbounding, with new designs springing up constantly. These days they are invariably electronic devices, although the old mechanical Halda is still used – and some say it is by far the best. Whether electronic or mechanical, they should take their readings from a non-driven wheel, so wheelspin can be ignored. Mechanical meters are arguably the most dependable, as the electronic meters depend on readings from sensors, which have been known to suffer damage on rough roads. However, if fitted properly, they can give years of reliable service. The most popular meters are Haldas, Terratrips, Microtrips and Brantz. Simple basic meters should cost under £100, whilst sophisticated units giving supplementary information, such as road speed, average speed and time of day, can cost hundreds.

Clock. As stage rallies refer to the actual time of day, an accurate clock, or watch, is an essential piece of equipment. Here again, there are many timepieces on the market, both electronic and mechanical, costing a fortune – but basic digital watches with stopwatch facility can be bought for under £10. A watch with the facility to freeze time displayed whilst continuing to run unseen is the ideal, so you can freeze the time you crossed a stage flying finish, then refer back to 'standard' time for the rally at the press of a button.

Crash helmet. You are required by RAC regulations to wear a helmet during a special stage. The Blue Book details the approved standards of helmets for different levels of rallying, whilst the FISA Yellow Book details the international requirements. Never buy the first helmet you see; choose one that fits snugly and feels comfortable – you will be wearing it for a long time. Also, consider its weight, as your head will be flung about on a stage and the heavier the helmet, the greater will be the strain on your neck muscles. A full-face helmet generally weighs more than an open-face helmet. If you wear glasses, take that into consideration as well – you may need to take them off for cleaning whilst still wearing the helmet.

Intercom. Travelling in a rally car along a special stage and wearing helmets makes it difficult to communicate with your driver. You can try shouting, but after a couple of stages you won't have anything left to shout with! An intercom eases the problem. Again, there are plenty to choose from at a price, or you can make one yourself. The ideal intercom is one which has no physical connection between the two sets, so if you are out of the car and wearing helmets you can still communicate. Whichever type you choose, make sure it has a simple push connector which can be split easily if you need to exit the car in a hurry. Also mount the amplifier box somewhere within reach when wearing seat belts, but don't allow the leads to foul any of the driver's controls.

Other specialized equipment could include a fluorescent marker pen for picking out important notes in road books (controls and cautions) and clauses in regulations. Time cards should be fixed to a clipboard and a spare pen carried for marshals' use. Stage time check sheets are also useful for keeping records of your own times and those of other competitors. As you progress to higher-status events, so does the volume of your paperwork. You will eventually need to produce a schedule for your service crew, detailing when and where to be, what tyres are required and how much fuel to put in the car. You should also take 1:50 000 and 1:250 000 scale maps for yourself and the service crew – having marked the service crew's route on the map for them; in return, they will make sure they have the kettle boiling when you arrive, ready for a brew!

Reading the route
It is doubtful whether you will be able to read the roads to your driver without having plotted the entire route beforehand. You can complete the route by simply using the road book, but every junction is not detailed, neither are the bad bends! If you have the time available, always transfer the route from the road book to 1:50 000 scale maps. Road books are OK if you don't have a problem with the car and can potter along road sections at a steady pace, but if you hit a problem and need to speed things up a bit, you can't beat reading the road to your driver. It allows him to drive both quicker and safer. If you break down on a road section, it also helps to be able to give a map reference of the location to your service crew. When using a road book, always tick off each instruction as you reach it, so at any given point you know exactly where you are.

On special stages you can still be of help to your driver, despite not knowing all of the hazards. From the road book, you will be able to tell him in advance of junctions, detailed bends and cautions, by referring to your tripmeter. Bearing in mind he will only be looking at the road immediately in front of the car, by looking into the distance, you might spot something worth mentioning like a 'caution' board, a bridge or a hairpin bend. The route through special stages is usually arrowed. A warning arrow is placed before the junction (usually on the left-hand side of the road), followed by two more arrows, one either side of the road forming a 'gate', with a single confirmation arrow on the correct road after the

The inside of a stage rally car with everything to hand. At the side of the seat is a handy pocket for storing time cards and maps. The tripmeter and map lights are easily reached, as are the battery cut-off and fire extinguisher switches. A radio is neatly tucked away so that it can be used by either driver or co-driver. (*Large*)

Arrows like these are usually in bright or fluorescent colours to make them stand out against the background. A warning arrow is placed before the corner or junction, then a pair of arrows form a 'gate' to drive through at the actual hazard. Brushwood can be seen behind the right-hand arrow, used to block off a road not to be used, whilst just visible is a length of light-coloured fluorescent tape strung across the front of the trailer to make it more noticeable. For the same reason, paint has been splashed on the logs jutting out on the inside of the bend. (*Large*)

junction. Whenever you see an arrow, tell the driver which way it is pointing.

Stage arrowing is a really old chestnut. Some Stage Commanders simply place the arrows to indicate straight on, left, or right, whilst others position the arrows to indicate the sharpness of the junction. A well-organized rally should have a constant arrowing system, whether good or bad! The same goes for Tulip diagrams of stages, which should be numbered both in the road book and physically at the junction.

There is nothing to stop you using the map whilst on a stage, but not all Forestry Commission roads are marked. It may be worth following the route to begin with, then, if it reads accurately, try calling a few bends to your driver – if he approves, carry on. Good map reading in forests can give a driver tremendous confidence, particularly on roads with a number of blind crests. It can help spot those horrifying phenomena known as firebreaks. These occur where a strip of land the width of a road has been left unplanted to act as a firebreak to arrest a forest fire. They invariably occur on the blind side of crests in the road. With no navigator, the driver would imagine that the road carried straight on; what follows is then either a time-consuming excursion down a rough muddy track, or at worse a collision

with something solid! By following the road on the map, you should be able to spot a deceptive firebreak.

On airfield stages, the 'gate' arrows could be on either side of a runway, some 30 metres apart. You will have to be the driver's other pair of eyes, particularly on these tests. You should be looking for unexpected kerbs, gateposts and junctions turning into narrow (and maybe unsurfaced) tracks. Many of these stages may be lapped a number of times, passing a split-off junction to the stage finish. It is not good enough just to tell your driver the number of times to pass the junction going, say, straight on, then expect him to remember to turn off after the right number. You should keep a check of that yourself – preferably by writing the number of laps down and crossing them off as you complete them. The same applies for forest stages with split junctions – drivers are creatures of habit and if they passed the junction turning left the first time, you can bet your bottom dollar they'll do it again when you really want to turn right. Once past it, there is no turning back; traffic on special stages is strictly one way only – and that includes reversing! So, if you overshoot the stage finish line, you should get out and walk back, telling your driver not to move an inch.

7

Your First Stage Rally

Competing on a special stage rally for the first time can be a harrowing experience, even for hardened road rally navigators. The essence of speed, timing and staying on the correct route is augmented by new rules and regulations, both written and unwritten. The previously successful navigator becomes a fledgling co-driver, in peril of becoming that proverbial 'sack of spuds'.

The paperwork for a co-driver is a little more complex than for a navigator and the role of office manager is taken on. To give an idea of what to expect on a special stage rally, the 1983 Gwynedd Rally is taken as an example. It forms part of the RAC National Championship and can be considered the pinnacle of club rallying. You will probably be introduced to stage rallying by a small single-venue event – an excellent way of finding your feet in a new branch of the sport. But the more serious events will follow the format of the Gwynedd.

After receiving a set of Regs, the entry form should be returned quickly, with as much seeding information as possible. Your start number is much more important on forest events than on tarmac rallies, as the special stage surfaces deteriorate with the passage of cars. The higher your start number, the less rough the roads will be and your times should be quicker. This is the first round of the Championship, so the organizers will probably know little of your driver's capabilities – that seeding information is vital to them as well.

The moment you receive confirmation of your entry is the time to book hotel rooms for the entire crew, which includes the service crew. Rally HQ is an ideal place to stay as there will invariably be a specially lowered price for rooms over the weekend of the rally and the hotel staff will be switched-on to the needs of rally folk. Also, if you have been lucky enough to attract a sponsor, you need to apply to the RAC MSA for an Advertising Permit, allowing the rally car to be painted in the sponsor's livery. The permit takes the form of an adhesive-backed disc, which must be attached to the vehicle dashboard; a separate one is required for each competing car of a team – and they are not cheap!

Car preparation is usually left in the hands of the driver or his mechanics, but you should keep an eye on things and make sure any spare parts are ordered on time, well in advance of the event. You should also check that your seating position is correct and that you can easily reach the controls of tripmeters, stopwatches and intercom whilst tightly belted in place. A door pocket will be a useful asset and it is imperative that you practise a system of changing a punctured wheel. Also, check the position of fire extinguishers and know how to release them from their mountings *and* how to use them.

Stage rally cars will invariably be more spartan inside than a road rally car and items such as jackets and bags will have to be carefully stowed away. Because the underside of the cars take such a pounding from forest roads, the exhaust system is mounted near the car floor and accordingly there may be areas inside the car which will get extremely hot – certainly hot enough to melt a plastic holdall bag or jacket. Make sure that your helmets are stowed safely out of harm's way, but also in an accessible position when wearing seat belts.

During the last couple of weeks before the rally, you should be looking around for information of the route. Read reports of last year's event and chat to fellow co-drivers about likely tricky spots on the stages. Bad corners and jumps should be marked by a caution sign (usually a '!'), but you should ask about any well-known firebreaks that could catch you out. You should also seek the advice of a more

FOREWORD

In introducing the first round of the 1983 National Stage Rally Championship, we welcome you to two events - the 'Gwynedd Rally' and the 'Gwynedd Bach Rally'. The latter sees the innovation of a Clubman's championship which we hope will prove as interesting and successful as the National one, which owes its continued existance to the generous support of Shell Oils.

As organisers of this event, we are particularly grateful to Mr. Geoffrey Lofthouse and the Imperial Hotel, Llandudno, for the support given to the Gwynedd Rally. The format follows that of previous years with the added attraction of some excellent Stages that have not been available to us for some time.

Please submit your entries as soon as possible and we shall look forward to meeting everyone at scrutineering and signing-on.

Jim Jones, John Robinson, Richard Yates, Dafydd Edwards.

PAST WINNERS

As a Road Event	As a Stage Event
1970 Roy Fidler/Barry Hughes	1975 Terry Brown/Ednyfed Morgan
1971 Roy Fidler/Barry Hughes	1976 Tony Fall/Mike Broad
1972 Vicki Lambert/Tony Goulding	1977 Nigel Roakey/Derick Tucker
1973 Russell Brookes/Neil Wilson	1978 Malcolm Wilson/Ron Palmer
	1979 Jimmy McRae/Mike Nicholson
	1980 Peter Clarke/Phil Boland
	1981 Russell Brookes/Mike Broad
	1982 Terry Kaby/Rob Arthur

ACKNOWLEDGEMENTS

The organisers gratefully acknowledge the assistance and support of the following:

SHELL OILS	VAUGHAN ALCOCK, RALLY TIME
RAC MOTOR SPORTS ASSOCIATION LTD.	PUGH'S GARAGE, DOLGELLAU
THE FORESTRY COMMISSION	GLYNDWR MILK BAR, DOLGELLAU
NORTH WALES POLICE	FARMERS MARTS, DOLGELLAU
SNOWDONIA NATIONAL PARK	WEST SHORE GARAGE, LLANDUDNO
IMPERIAL HOTEL, LLANDUDNO	WATERLOO HOTEL, BETWS—Y—COED
ABERCONWY BOROUGH COUNCIL	GEELER ARMS, PENTREFOELAS
DICK TAYLOR AND MERCURY RADIO	

1983 GWYNEDD NATIONAL RALLY
&
GWYNEDD BACH RESTRICTED RALLY

Organised by the Caernarfonshire & Anglesey Motor Club
with the Imperial Hotel, Llandudno

SUPPLEMENTARY REGULATIONS PART 2

18 TIMETABLE OF RALLY

Monday, 24th January, 1983	Entries open
Monday, 21st February, 1983	Entries close at normal fee
Monday, 28th February, 1983	Entries close at normal fee plus surcharge
Monday, 7th March, 1983	Final instructions posted
Friday, 11th March, 1983, 18.30 hrs	Rally HQ opens for documentation and scrutineering for both events.
Saturday,12th March, 1983	Documentation and scrutineering for Restricted event and this by appointment only.
Saturday, 12th March, 1983, 08.00 hrs	Gwynedd Rally starts
Following the National Rally	Start of Gwynedd Bach Rally
Saturday, 12th March, 1983, 17.00 hrs	Rally finishes
Saturday, 12th March, 1983, 21.00 hrs	Provisional results posted
Saturday, 12th March, 1983, 22.00 hrs	Presentation of awards

19 ANNOUNCEMENT

The Caernarvonshire and Anglesey Motor Club will promote a dual permit Stage rally on Saturday, 12th March, 1983, the events to be known as the 'Gwynedd Rally' and the 'Gwynedd Bach Rally'.

The Gwynedd Rally is a qualifying round of the Shell Oils/Autosport RAC National Rally Championship, the Ford Escort Turbo Rally Championship and the A.N.W.C.C. Stage Rally Championship.

The Gwynedd Bach Rally is a qualifying round of the Shell Clubman's Championship and the A.N.W.C.C. Stage Rally Championship.

19a ELIGIBILITY - for National Event see paragraph 2.

Gwynedd Bach — open to all holders of a Restricted or higher status competition licence issued by the RACMSA valid for the event and who are also either:-
(i)   Fully paid-up members of the C & A Motor Club,   OR
(ii)   Registered competitors in the   "   ..   ..   "   OR
(iii) Registered competitors in the A.N.W.C.C. Stage Rally Championship.

20 AUTHORISATION

RAC	Permit	No	(i)	....
RAC	Permit	No	(ii)	....

DoE	Authorisation	No.	....

Shell Oils/Autosport RAC Championship Permit No. CH/2084
Ford Escort Turbo Rally Championship Permit No. CH/2086

21 START & FINISH

The event will start and finish in Llandudno and Rally Headquarters will be at the Imperial Hotel. (M.R. 115/785½822½)

22 ROUTE

The route will be on Ordnance Survey 1:50,000 Maps 115,116,124,and 125. Total distance of the National event will be 250 miles, of which at least 70 miles will be on special stages. Total distance of the Restricted event will be 150 of which at least 40 miles will be on special stages.

23 AWARDS

(i) Gwynedd Rally
(a) General Classification

1st Driver	Milburn Trophy and replica
1st Co-Driver	D.G. Jones Trophy and replica

(b) Class Awards

1st Class A1	A challenge trophy and replica
1st Class A2	National Benzole Trophy and replica
1st Class A3	R.A. Yates Trophy and replica
1st Class A4	A challenge trophy and replica
1st Class B1	Elfed Cup and replica
1st Class B2	J.C. Robinson Rose Bowl and replica
1st Class B3	Uniflo Gwynedd Trophy and replica

2nd in each class: awards subject to 10 entries in the class.
3rd in each class: awards subject to 15 entries in the class.

Winners of General Classification Awards will not be eligible for Class Awards.

(c) Other Awards

i.   For the best performance by a crew, both being members of the C & A Motor Club before 1st December, 1982, and who do not win one of the abovementioned awards.
ii. For the best performance by a Clwyd Vale M.C. entry: A challenge trophy presented by Clwyd Vale Motor Club.
iii. To the competitor who, in the opinion of a panel appointed by the organisers, sets the most meritorious performance during the rally, irrespective of finishing position.
(d) Shell Oils/Autosport Trophy presented to:
i.   The highest placed registered driver and highest placed registered co-driver.
ii. The highest placed registered Group A driver and the highest placed co-driver in a Group A car.

(ii) Gwynedd Bach Rally
The Menai Cup and replicas to the winning crew and outright awards to second and third crews overall subject to the number of entries received.
Additional awards may be notified in the Final Instructions.
Named trophies remain the property of the C & A Motor Club and must be returned when requested.

24 ENTRIES

Normal closing date for entries is Monday, 21st February, 1983.
Entry list closes at normal fee plus surcharges on Monday, 28th February, 1983. All late entries will be subject to an administration fee of £10. The standard entry fee for the Gwynedd Rally is £120 which includes one service pack. The standard entry fee for the Gwynedd Bach Rally is £68 which includes one service pack.
All entries must be made on the official entry form and accompanied by the full fee. The organisers regret that entries cannot be accepted in any other form. The maximum entry for the National event is 120 plus reserves. The organisers reserve the right to cancel the event if less than 70 entries are received. The maximum entry for the Restricted event is 60 plus reserves.
See SR5 in Part 1 for conditions applying to withdrawn entries.
Reserves who pass scrutineering and sign-on, but who are not allocated a place, will have the whole of their entry fee refunded.
The Entries Secretary, to whom all entries must be sent, is:
Mrs. Barbara Jones, 36 Kearsley Drive, Rhyl, Clwyd. Tel: 0745 - 53014

25 OFFICIALS

RAC Steward: T.B.A.
Club Stewards: David Stevenson and John Brown.
Clerks of the Course: Jim Jones and John Robinson
Secretary of Meeting: Dafydd Edwards, Lliwedd, 92 Lon Hedydd, Llanfairpwll, Gwynedd.
Chief Marshal: Richard Yates, 60 Trafford Park, Penrhyn Bay, Llandudno, (0492-44291)
Assistant Chief Marshal: Ian Hughes
Chief Scrutineer: W. Glyn Jones
Eligibility Scrutineer: T.B.A.
RAC Timekeeper: Vaughan Alcock
Chief Timekeeper: Peter Roberts
Safety Officer: Mike Crook
Results: Tynemouth Computer Results Service
Results Manager: Alun M. Hughes
Press Officer: Brian Rainbow, 2 The Beeches, Harbury, Warwicks. CV33 9LW.
              Tel: 0926 612415 (Home) 0926 32525 Ex. 5092 (Business)

26 AMMENDMENTS TO SUPPLEMENTARY REGS. PART 1

SR 6 - The minimum target time for a special stage will be 10 minutes.

27 ADDITIONAL INFORMATION

Accommodation -
The Imperial Hotel, Llandudno (0492 - 77466) is again the headquarters of the Gwynedd Rally and offers a special tariff to all connected with the event. The basic rate is £12.95 per person for bed & breakfast and you are advised to use the reservation form enclosed with these regulations. Supplements for extras are £1 for bathroom, £1 for single room (£3 with bath). In addition to the normal restaurant and 'Speakeasy' facilities, there will be a hot/cold buffet and early (6.30 am) breakfast on the Saturday.

experienced co-driver as to whether OS 1:50 000 scale maps are accurate for the forest roads in the area.

During the week before the rally, you will receive a set of Final Instructions, indicating your start number and start time and detailing the timetable of the pre-rally formalities, *i.e.* noise check, scrutineering, *parc ferme*, documentation and start procedure. Your next task is to prepare duplicate sets of documents for each team member.

Relevant clauses in the event Regs and Final Instructions should be marked for the attention of the service crew and driver. Details of the accommodation booked and the location of the hotel

 Shell Oils

 GWYNEDD RALLY

Organized by:
Caernarvonshire & Anglesey Motor Club
with the Imperial Hotel, Llandudno

FINAL INSTRUCTIONS TO COMPETITORS

R.A.C. PERMIT NO. RAL 1203/3   AUTHORISATION NO. (At Start)

Your number is ....   You will start at .... hours.

If you are unable to start please inform the Entries Secretary as soon as possible.

Phone RHYL (0745) 53014
(up to 11.00 pm Thursday)

N.B.   Regular competitors should please note that there are different arrangements for Scrutineering, etc., this year and the instructions should be read carefully.

All competition vehicles must be off-loaded in Builder Street car park (see enclosed map) and trailers may be left there during the event. Trailers will NOT BE ALLOWED into the Start area.

Please observe the sequence:- NOISE TEST - SCRUTINEERING - PARC FERME - DOCUMENTATION.

NOISE TEST On arrival, and before reporting for Scrutineering or Signing-on, please report to the Noise Official at Builder Street Car park at 781815. The Noise Control will be open from 18.30 hours to 22.00 hours on Friday, 11th March. On completing the Test you will be issued with a card to be produced at Scrutineering, Start Area and Signing-on.

SCRUTINEERING PROCEDURE Scrutineering will take place at West Shore Garage (see enclosed map). Service cars should park in the Builder Street car park.

Trade Service vehicles will be parked in the Builder Street car park.

Door panels are being provided by Shell Oils and are to be fixed to the front doors. These will be fixed when cars enter parc ferme, as will the event side plates and decals. Competition numbers will be on sale at scrutineering and should be fixed in position on the abovementioned panels.

Championship contenders should display current decals as required by the regulations.

SIGNING ON will take place at Rally HQ in the Imperial Hotel on Friday evening.

Registered entrants in the Shell Oils Autosport National Rally Championship should ensure that they also sign the Championship signing-on sheets.

ROADBOOK and SERVICE PACK will be issued at Rally HQ when all formalities have been completed. Your card must be signed by the Noise Official, Scrutineer, Start Area Marshal and Secretary before the Roadbook will be issued. No car will be allowed to leave the official car park after its crew has received the Roadbook.

Crews must sign for their Service Packs and give the make, colour and registration number of their Service Vehicle on the enclosed application form. The Service Plate must be displayed inside the windscreen at all times during the event unless the competing car has retired.

SHELL FORUM In conjunction with the Rally, the Shell Forum will take place in the ballroom at The Imperial Hotel at 8.00 p.m. on Friday evening. All competitors, service crews, etc., are welcome.

START AREA will be open from 07.15 hours on Saturday.

STAGE SURFACE The first Special Stage is one mile from the Start and has tarmac surface. There is a Service Area immediately after this Stage.

TYRES - Racing 'slicks' will not be permitted as they are illegal on public roads which must be traversed to get to and from Stages.

AMENDMENTS TO S.R.s

SR 20   RAC Permit No. RAL 1203/3

SR 4   CLASSES
Due to lack of entries in classes A1, A2, A3 & A4, these cannot be run seperately and for the purposes of the event classes A1 and A2 will be amalgamated, as will classes A3 and A4.

SR 23   AWARDS
(b) Class Awards.
1st class A1/A2 combined - National Benzole Trophy & replicas.
1st class A3/A4 combined - R.A.Yates Trophy & replicas.

Due to the number of entries received for each class, Class Awards will be as follows:-
Classes A1/A2, B1 and B2 - Award to 1st in class only.
Class A3/A4   - Awards to 1st & 2nd.
Class B3   - Awards to 1st, 2nd, 3rd, 4th & 5th.

SR25   OFFICIALS   RAC Steward: Mr C.B.F.Belton. Eligibility Scrutineer: Mr G.Ward
Chief Medical Officer: Dr. I.W.Jones. Noise Official: David Thomas

The following are Judges of Fact regarding infringements of noise and servicing regs.
Phil Roe,   Peter Roe,   Jim Thomson,   Ken Jones,   Mike Crook,   Ray Carlisle.

SR 22   ROUTE In addition to the maps specified, sheet 135 shows approx. ½ mile of main road to a Stage Start but the Roadbook provides adequate information.

EVENING MEALS on Friday and Saturday are available at the Imperial Hotel in the Speakeasy Bar, the restaurant or as a cold buffet.

AFTER THE RALLY - A 'Disco' at the Imperial Hotel for all associated with the event.

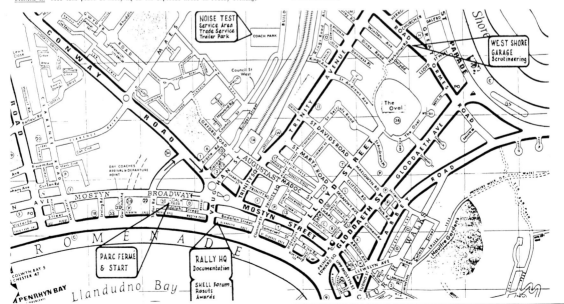

can easily be given by photocopies of a town street guide, together with a time of arrival for the team. The service crew will probably have the job of towing the rally car to the start, and a suggested parking place for the trailer should be given to them in addition to any other requests such as filling fuel cans at a specific garage.

Aim to arrive early for the rally and book into the hotel before doing anything else. It has been known for rooms to be double-booked! Make a list of room numbers and which team members will be occupying them, then arrange for the hotel staff to give a morning call at a specific time. The Gwynedd starts at 08.00, so plenty of time should be allowed for, making certain that breakfast will be available early on the Saturday morning. Your next job should be to locate the various sites for noise check, trailer park, scutineering and documentation – and in this case the overnight *parc ferme*. This is a closed parking area for competing cars only, where no work can be carried out on them. They are generally used on International rallies, but as in this case, they can crop up on any event. Once placed in *parc ferme*, a car cannot leave before a specified time and the crew is not permitted to return to the car in the meantime. Whilst waiting for the team to arrive, it is not a bad idea to make sure that food will be available somewhere late into the evening.

The trailer park is at the noise check location, so be there early to wait for your car to arrive unless you are travelling down together. Have a look at a few other cars passing through the noise check before you take your car in. On this occasion, there are a number of trade support vehicles in the area, so if you have an agreement with one of them, take advantage of it. Park close by and use their floodlights to help with any work on the car – it will probably be dark when you arrive on Friday evening.

At the noise check you will be handed a documentation card, which will be needed for scrutineering and signing-on. After the noise check, take the car to scrutineering, then return to the trade service area to carry out any last-minute jobs (there will invariably be last-minute jobs!). The Final Instructions tell you that the first special stage is on tarmac and only a short distance from the start, so it will be no good fitting forest tyres when taking the car to *parc ferme*. If you have a choice of tarmac tyres, opt for a tyre in the middle of the range. Weather conditions will no doubt change and the organizers will allow tyres to be changed before the first stage the following morning, but just in case a last-minute panic befalls the team, a tyre which can cope with both dry and wet roads should be fitted if possible.

At scrutineering, the officials will check for items detailed in the RAC MSA Vehicle Regulations (in the Blue Book) and helmets will be inspected for eligibility, together with an Advertising Permit if relevant. When you are satisfied that everything is in order (and the intercom is working), the car should be driven to *parc ferme*, where door plates will be fitted and competition numbers stuck in place, together with any advertising decals the organizers may require to satisfy their own event backers. If you are registered for a championship, decals for that series may also be needed.

On the larger rallies, scrutineering is generally in more civilized surroundings, just as it is here. (*Lynord*)

An example of a typical documentation card.

GWYNEDD RALLY

No. _____

NOISE OFFICIAL _____

SCRUTINEER _____

SECRETARY _____

CAR PARK _____

Exchange completed card for Roadbook.

Only when you are completely satisfied that everything is in order should you walk from *parc ferme* – you won't be allowed back in until the rally organizer decrees. The next job is documentation, even though the temptation to eat will be strong. It is always best if the co-driver handles all the paperwork, which includes Competition Licences, insurance certificates, entrant's licences, championship registration cards and the documentation card issued at the noise check. You may also, as in this case, have to register your service

'barges' with the organizers. When you have successfully signed-on, you will receive a road book detailing the rally route, a set of time cards and any amendments to the regulations already issued. There will also be an Official Noticeboard where further information is displayed regarding any changes. Before leaving documentation, make absolutely sure you have everything you are supposed to have by checking through the items with an official – a missed route amendment at this point could be catastrophic. Now it's time to eat.

'You can't do that!' Top co-driver Roger Freeman receives an ear-bending from one of the officials at signing-on. In the background is the Official Noticeboard, where amendments and organizing permits are displayed. There should also be a list of the names of Judges of Fact on display. (*Lynord*)

After eating, your next job is to plan a service schedule for the mechanics to follow. A small-scale 1:250 000 OS map is ideal to draw out a route for the service crew. The Gwynedd Rally road book includes a route for service crews to follow, so it is a simple matter to transfer this to a map. You should indicate your estimated arrival time at each service area (usually allowing 15 minutes or so extra travelling time, just in case the mechanics themselves have a problem, and not forgetting that it takes time to load and unload a service van) and show how long you have at each service point. This needs to be supplemented by a written schedule, which should include details of which types of tyre are needed and roughly how much fuel will be required. Planning a service schedule for an International is an extremely complex operation and is dealt with in a later chapter.

Before you turn in for the night, you should plan to lay out all of your paperwork in the correct order, ready for a quick start the next morning. Although a road book and tripmeter are adequate for navigating

around most special stage rally routes, it is never a bad idea to plot the route on 1:50 000 OS maps as well – but rules don't allow the route of special stages to be marked on the maps. There may be checks along the route, where crew and car are searched for pace notes, and if stage routes are marked on your maps they constitute pace notes. That offence will not only see your exclusion from the rally, but the RAC MSA will undoubtedly suspend your Competition Licence for a minimum of three months.

It is always a good idea to take your own alarm clock with you and it is your responsibility in the morning to make sure everyone else in your team is awake at the right time. Arrange to meet for breakfast about an hour before the rally start time, where you can explain the service schedule to the mechanics. The organizers have asked for you to be ready in the *parc ferme* 15 minutes before your due start time and have allowed service crews to enter the *parc* to change tyres. The service crew is dispatched to various tasks, whilst you and your driver finish

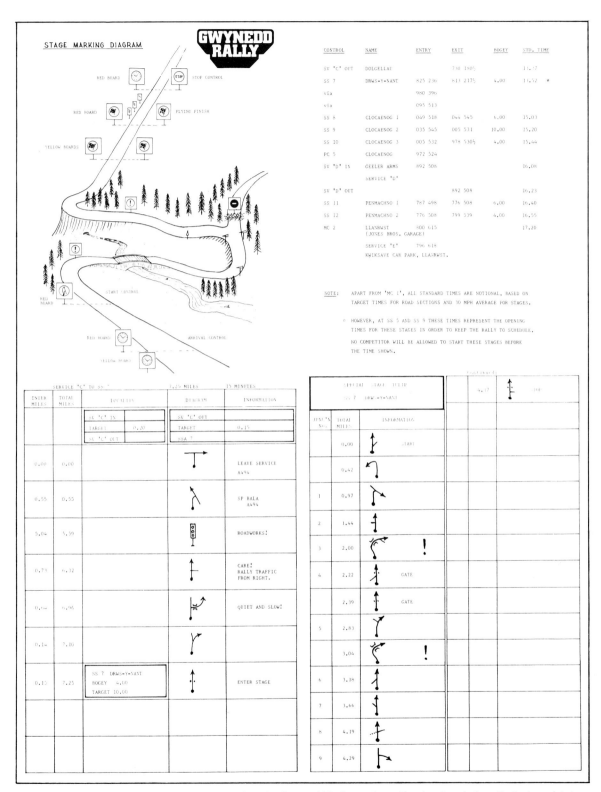

Shown here are examples of the road book pages from the Gwynedd Rally together with a drawing of a hypothetical special stage showing where control boards and stage arrows are usually placed.

breakfast (it could be the last time you eat before the rally finish), then walk to the rally car, where the correct tyres have already been fitted.

Before anything else, your driver should start the car. If it fails, you have at least a 15-minute period to sort things out! Check that all the necessary rally plates and sponsor's decals are in place. Then, you are called to a holding control, which dispatches cars in groups of five to the actual start outside the rally HQ hotel. Whilst queuing at the holding control (or at the start control) you should synchronize your watch or clock with the marshal's clock – this will be your lifeline for the entire event. Check that the marshal fills in your time card correctly and that your road book is at the right page, with an OS map folded to show the correct portion you are about to traverse.

Target time for the first road section is five minutes. This is shown on both your time card and at the top of the relevant page in the road book. You should add this time to your scheduled start time to calculate your scheduled arrival time at the next stage arrival control. You establish your scheduled start time by referring to the rally standard start time (08.00) and adding your competition number multiplied by the interval between cars (in this case a one-minute interval). So for car number 1, the start time is 08.01 and for car number 73, the start time is 09.13. At the rally start, you should zero the tripmeter, as each individual section is detailed with its own total distance.

The first stage is only a few hundred yards away from the rally start, but you have to wait for your correct scheduled time before booking in – in the meantime you should have fitted your helmet and handed your driver his helmet. After the arrival control, all rules of timing go straight out of the window as you enter what is called 'dead' time – your fate is then in the hands of the organizers, specifically the individual Stage Commander. If there has been a delay on the stage, he may decide to hold cars at the stage start until he is satisfied all is OK to restart proceedings, or he may close-up any gaps in the entry and expect you to start the stage on the next available whole minute. For the latter reason, you should present yourselves at the stage start ready to tackle it immediately, i.e. with belts fitted and helmets on. If you are not ready to start the stage, you will be allotted a start time, but you will not be permitted to move the car until your belts and helmets are properly fitted. Your trip should be zeroed at the stage start control, not the arrival control.

In the case of the Gwynedd, the first stage is around the Great Orme and can be read from the map without fear of missing a junction. A co-driver 'navigating' his driver in this way can shave seconds from a stage time.

At the end of the stage, you will see a pair of yellow boards indicating the approach of the flying finish. The flying finish itself is marked by a pair of red boards either side of the road and indicates the position to which you are being timed. As you pass the boards, the stage finish marshals will stop their clock and write that time on your time card in hours, minutes and seconds. Immediately after the flying finish boards, your driver should be slowing down, ready to stop at the finish control. If, however, you overshoot the stop line, *don't* reverse the car back; get out and walk back as it is an offence to drive against rally traffic. At the stop control, your tripmeter should be zeroed ready to start the next road section.

Always check the marshal's clock against your own watch (which you should have stopped as you passed the flying finish boards); if there is a discrepancy of an odd second, forget it, but if it is greater than five seconds complain about it – but only of course if it is not in your favour! If the marshal's clock is still running, then definitely complain, as it should have been 'frozen' at your finish time. In this case, you should ask the marshals to look at the time on your own watch and to record that on their check sheets, so you have evidence of it at the rally finish – part way through an event is not the time to start querying stage penalties.

The target time to the next control, Service 'A' In, is five minutes. To calculate your scheduled arrival time, add the target time to your stage finish time in hours and minutes, but omitting the seconds – road sections are timed to the previous whole minute. You are given a target time for the service area of 10 minutes, which is added to your arrival time to give your scheduled time at Service 'A' Out. At the top of each road book page where a section starts, there is a panel for entering your own times. You should, however, only enter the time that appears on your time card. If you fill the times in before hand, i.e. predicting your time at Service 'A' Out, you may inadvertently forget about any lateness (although penalty-free) incurred at the service area. For instance, you may have run over your service time by a couple of minutes. In itself this carries no penalty except being accumulated towards your Maximum Permitted Lateness, but if you had entered your planned time out of service in the appropriate space at the top of the page, you will have calculated a time two minutes early at the following control, which *will* be penalized.

En route to the next special stage, you have to visit a passage control, where a time card will be collected. Before handing in the time card, transfer the last time over to the next card, i.e. SV 'A' Out. As the day goes on, you will have more of these card collection points along the route. Tick off the relevant

| CONTROL | TIMEKEEPERS | | | | | | FOR OFFICIAL USE ONLY |
	SIGNATURE	HRS	MIN	SEC	PREVIOUS CAR NO.	TARGET	
SS 6 FINISH	B/FWD	13	15				—
PC 4	J.						✓
SV 'C' IN(MC 2)	S.E.F.	13	40			25	—
SV 'C' OUT	RB	14	00			20	—
SS 7 ARRIVAL	S.Q.	14	18			15	3
START	S.R.	14	20		12		—
FINISH	D.H.	14	27	05		10	7.05
SS 8 ARRIVAL						1-03	
START							
FINISH						12	
SS 9 ARRIVAL						5	
START							
FINISH						20	
SS 10 ARRIVAL						4	
START							
FINISH						10	

Time Card No. **5**

GWYNEDD RALLY

TIME CARD NO. COMPETITOR NO.

HAND IN THIS CARD AT PC 5 AND ENSURE THAT YOUR SS 10 FINISH TIME IS
TRANSFERRED TO TIME CARD NO. 6

GWYNEDD BACH RALLY COMPETITORS HAND IN THIS CARD AT SV 'C' IN (MC 2)
TOGETHER WITH THE DAMAGE DECLARATION ON TIME CARD NO. 6

This time card shows a late arrival at SS7 Arrival by 3 minutes – this will be added to the penalty-free lateness total in calculating whether or not the crew goes over MPL.

junctions in the road book as you pass them, so if you become distracted – say by a couple of blondes hitch-hiking – you can refer straight away to your next instruction. On the way, your driver will invariably be asking questions about what is coming up: How long is the next stage? How many miles to the next service? How long is the next service? You should be *au fait* with this sort of information.

The next stage is Beddgelert, 6.1 miles long and with 21 junctions; it is doubtful that you will be able to follow it on the map. As you start the stage, you should again zero the trip and start your watch, calling out the junctions to your driver and looking for anything untoward he may not have noticed.

```
                    GWYNEDD RALLY 1983
                    RESULTS - PAGE 1
                                            POSITION
            CREW                      CLASS TOTAL  CLASS  OVERALL

   2 George Hill/Ronald Varley      Chevette      7  Head gasket
   3 Bill Dobie/Steve Fellows       Ascona 400    7  79:51      1       1
   5 Phil Collins/Lynn Jenkins      Ascona 400    7  80:22      2       2
   6 Donald Heggie/Bryan Harris     Escort        7  Rear Suspension
   7 Graham Elsmore/Alyn Edwards    TR8           7  83:37      8       8
   8 John Brown/Dave Nicholson.     Escort        7  Electrical failure
   9 Terry Pankhurst/Roger Freeman  Escort        7  Half-shaft
  10 Nigel Worswick/Stuart Derry    Escort        7  Broken oil pipe
  11 Roger Chilman/Bryan Thomas     Escort        7  82:20      6       6
  12 Jeff Churchill/Roger Evans     Escort        7  84:54     10      10
  14 Darryl Weidner/Doug Hart       Quattro       7  81:36      3       3
  15 George Marshall/Ken Wilson     Chevette      7  81:57      5       5
  16 Phil Taylor/Pauline Taylor     Escort        7  85:48     11      11
  17 David Llewellin/Martin James   Escort        7  81:51      4       4
  18 Roy Cathcart/Harold Montgomery Escort        7  82:54      7       7
  20 Alun Edwards/Dave Read         Escort        7  84:02      9       9
  21 Kenneth McMillan/David Bole    Escort        7  RETIRED
  23 Tony Eaton/Stewart Anable      Escort        7  87:06     12      12
  24 Gary Hicks/Simon Warner        Violet        7  Crown wheel
  25 Gwyn Thomas/Wyn Morris         Chevette      7  RETIRED
  26 Trevor Smith/Brian Peacher     Escort Turbo  7  87:45     13      13
  27 Ian Tilke/Rick Smith           Escort Turbo  7  89:16     15      15
  28 George Forbes/Ian Anderson     Escort Turbo  7  Electrical failure
  29 Steve King/Andy Kay            Escort Turbo  7  94:38     17      26
  30 Philip Wilks/John Robinson     Escort Turbo  7  88:40     14      14
  32 Mark Lovell/Peter Davis        Escort Turbo  7  Holed petrol tank
  33 Mervyn Coxon/Rowand Prentice   Escort Turbo  7  Accident
  34 David Mann/Jim Bowie           Escort Turbo  7  RETIRED
  36 Philip Atkinson/Derek Davies   Escort Turbo  7 105:40     20      31
  37 John Roberts/Kelvin Evans      TR8           7  93:11     16      21
  38 Richard Jenkins/Richard Ames   Escort Turbo  7  96:59     18      27
  39 David Sammons/Malcolm Andrews  Escort Turbo  7  Head gasket
  40 Steve Shaw/Christine Coward    Escort        7  Accident
  41 Clifford Spencer/David James   Nissan P910   3  92:05      1      19
  42 George Gass/Roy Herron         Ascona        3  Burst oil pipe
  43 Graham Hewitt/Melvyn Sparks    Escort        6  RETIRED
  44 Bob Jelley/Adrian Cooke        Chevette      7  Dropped Valve
  45 Chris Lloyd/Simon Gronow       Escort        6  RETIRED
  46 Ralph Lockey/John Millington   Sunny         5  RETIRED
  47 Drew Baxter/Ian Houghton       Avenger       6  RETIRED
  48 Malcolm Surgenor/Stephen Davies Sunbeam      2  90:14      2      17
  49 Brian Oswald/Steve Hall        Sunbeam       6  90:16      1      18
  50 Gordon Smith/Graham Batchelor  Sunbeam       6  RETIRED
  52 Mike May/Angela Lane           Escort        5 112:23      4      33
  54 David Maund/Philip Maund       Chevette      7  99:23     19      29
  56 Dean Senior/Philip Shaw        Levin         6  93:34      2      22
  59 David Williams/Wayne Goble     Escort        3  92:51      2      20
  60 Nev Styles/Mike Smith          Sunbeam       2  94:17      3      24
  61 Graham Brown/Paul Barton       Cooper S      5 103:07      3      30
  62 N.D. Talton/P.C. Gray          Rover SD1     7  Hit log pile
  63 Nigel Edwards/Patricia Edwards Sunbeam       6 110:55      3      32
  64 M. Clarke/M. Jeffrey           Sunbeam       2  90:08      1      16
  65 C.W. Roper/R.K. Ellis          Manta         3  97:28      3      28
  66 Andrew Seager/David Spafford   Escort        5  94:00      1      23
  67 John Burton/Chris Gilliver     Escort        5  94:31      2      25
```

Results are presented very differently on stage rallies. These have been calculated by computer and even include the reasons for various crews' retirement.

Again, tick junctions off as you pass them. Each instruction has a number alongside it in the road book which corresponds with a number physically shown at the junction – unless one of the cars in front has already wiped it out with a swing of its tail.

After a further stage (Maesgwm) there is a 20-minute service in Dolgellau, and it is there you have the task of checking other competitors' stage times and entering them on a record sheet. Times may be issued by the organizers, but they will probably be one or two stages out of date. Fellow co-drivers can usually supply stage times for other cars as well – always be truthful about your times, otherwise you will soon find the other co-drivers slipping you a few

```
                        GWYNEDD RALLY 1983
                        RESULTS - PAGE 3
                             STAGE                                          STAGE
        1      2      3      4      5      6      7      8      9         10     11     12    ROAD
        ORME        MAESGWM       GARTH'OG     DRWSYNANT    CLOCAENOG      CLOCAENOG   PENMACHNO
            BEDGELERT      MAWDDACH      PANTP'OG     CLOCAENOG              PENMACHNO
```

#	1	2	3	4	5	6	7	8	9	10	11	12	ROAD
2	3:01	8:06	6:50	3:01	10:19	9:55	4:40	6:43	11:26	4:34 Head gasket			
3	2:58	7:55	6:52	3:01	10:25	10:01	4:43	6:43	11:15	4:34	6:40	4:44	0:00
5	3:08	7:56	6:57	3:01	10:25	9:50	4:38	6:52	11:27	4:40	6:52	4:45	0:00
6	3:06	8:08	7:13	3:05	10:31	10:10	4:47	7:02	17:20	5:15 Rear Suspension			
7	3:06	8:26	7:16	3:06	10:48	10:22	4:50	7:01	11:53	4:52	6:57	5:00	0:00
8	3:10	8:02	7:01	3:02	Electrical failure					Electrical failure			
9	3:04	8:09	7:01	3:04	Half-shaft					Half-shaft			
10	2:57	8:12	Broken oil pipe							Broken oil pipe			
11	2:58	8:01	7:06	3:02	10:34	10:07	4:47	6:51	11:31	4:41	7:44	4:58	0:00
12	3:08	8:21	7:20	3:06	11:00	10:47	4:57	7:01	12:07	4:53	7:12	5:02	0:00
14	3:10	8:05	7:10	3:01	10:31	10:01	4:42	7:16	11:28	4:36	6:48	4:43	0:00
15	3:08	8:10	7:10	3:03	10:41	10:17	4:50	6:52	11:24	4:40	6:51	4:51	0:00
16	3:07	8:29	7:28	3:16	11:03	10:38	5:00	7:00	12:18	4:54	7:24	5:11	0:00
17	3:08	8:06	7:14	3:02	10:30	10:15	4:49	6:52	11:29	4:39	6:54	4:53	0:00
18	3:09	8:09	7:27	3:05	10:46	10:25	4:51	6:48	11:32	4:43	7:01	4:58	0:00
20	3:09	8:05	7:05	3:08	10:37	11:29	4:49	6:57	11:56	4:38	7:05	5:04	0:00
21	3:09	8:46	7:46	3:21	12:40	11:06	RETIRED			RETIRED			
23	3:23	8:35	7:49	3:16	11:12	10:54	5:03	7:08	12:05	4:54	7:31	5:16	0:00
24	3:22	8:33	7:51	3:18	11:26	11:06	Crown wheel			Crown wheel			
25	3:21	8:57	8:04	3:34	11:30	11:07	5:12	7:33	12:20	5:14 RETIRED			
26	3:26	8:33	7:40	3:17	11:25	11:01	5:08	7:19	12:20	4:59	7:15	5:12	0:00
27	3:13	8:56	8:02	3:23	11:31	11:02	5:17	7:27	12:24	5:03	7:38	5:20	0:00
28	3:24	8:42	Electrical failure							Electrical failure			
29	3:27	9:27	8:35	3:27	12:04	11:33	5:58	7:55	13:08	5:12	8:12	5:40	0:00
30	3:24	8:37	7:54	3:22	11:32	11:01	5:14	7:15	12:19	4:58	7:45	5:10	0:00
32	3:19	8:47	Holed petrol tank							Holed petrol tank			
33	3:15	9:04	10:42	4:14	Accident					Accident			
34	3:42	9:30	8:09	3:29	12:07	11:46	RETIRED			RETIRED			
36	3:29	9:26	8:35	3:29	12:09	11:41	5:34	11:57	18:18	6:44	8:20	5:58	0:00
37	3:16	9:06	7:56	3:19	11:33	11:09	5:13	7:36	12:22	5:00	7:27	5:14	4:00
38	3:25	12:00	7:55	4:01	12:09	11:26	6:08	7:34	12:46	5:10	8:34	5:51	0:00
39	3:48	10:20	9:35	3:50	13:10	13:07	Head gasket			Head gasket			
40	3:24	8:34	7:24	3:15	11:24	10:54	Accident			Accident			
41	3:34	8:37	7:46	3:17	13:32	11:17	5:25	7:39	12:43	5:12	7:39	5:24	0:00
42	3:18	8:26	Burst oil pipe							Burst oil pipe			
43	3:22	8:46	7:42	3:18	11:35	11:08	5:15	7:28	12:36	5:23 RETIRED			
44	3:08	8:18	7:19	3:08	11:00	10:47	Dropped Valve			Dropped Valve			
45	3:31	8:46	7:52	4:06	RETIRED					RETIRED			
46	3:26	8:32	12:00	6:12	RETIRED					RETIRED			
47	3:32	8:40	7:42	3:22	11:35	12:21	5:17	7:30	12:29	5:03 RETIRED			
48	3:27	8:44	7:46	3:24	11:51	11:23	5:20	7:31	12:43	5:06	7:43	5:16	0:00
49	3:32	8:47	8:49	3:21	11:45	10:58	5:12	7:26	12:23	5:06	7:32	5:25	0:00
50	3:45	9:05	8:10	3:31	RETIRED					RETIRED			
52	3:50	9:47	8:57	3:54	14:14	14:13	6:55	9:10	15:55	6:01	12:00	7:27	0:00
54	3:49	9:42	8:37	3:43	12:52	12:15	5:52	8:21	13:56	5:35	8:45	5:56	0:00
56	3:26	8:59	7:59	3:30	11:53	11:32	5:22	7:34	14:32	5:17	7:58	5:32	0:00
59	3:26	9:05	8:10	3:34	11:57	11:28	5:27	7:38	12:57	5:09	8:21	5:39	0:00
60	3:33	9:04	8:30	3:36	12:19	11:57	5:35	7:47	13:02	5:16	8:09	5:29	0:00
61	3:49	9:51	9:34	3:47	13:13	12:45	6:01	8:50	14:24	5:45	8:58	6:09	0:00
62	3:22	8:32	8:09	3:16	Hit log pile					Hit log pile			
63	3:16	8:51	7:50	3:30	18:00	11:32	5:20	12:00	18:18	10:00	8:37	5:41	0:00
64	3:28	8:50	7:49	3:20	11:45	11:24	5:17	7:25	12:29	5:08	7:53	5:20	0:00
65	3:40	9:13	8:14	3:45	12:24	12:28	5:40	7:55	13:16	5:36	8:33	6:05	0:00
66	3:35	9:17	7:53	3:28	11:57	11:40	5:30	7:55	13:16	5:32	8:12	5:45	0:00
67	3:26	12:00	9:04	3:27	11:49	11:26	5:23	7:42	12:44	5:04	8:00	5:26	0:00

suspect ones in return! Whether you keep your driver informed of the times and your position is a matter for your own judgment of the particular driver. Some drivers know their own capabilities, whilst others might try just that little bit too much and end up in a ditch. On a one-day 'sprint' type of rally, such as the Gwynedd, you can never say you are safe until the nearest man behind you is more than two minutes away – the time it takes to change a punctured tyre part way through a stage. On this type of event two minutes could well span the entire top 10 at the finish.

At the time of year the Gwynedd is run, auxiliary lights should never really be needed, but if you were running at the back of the field and there had been delays at stage starts, it would be a good idea to fit them for the final pair of stages – just in case.

After completing the final stage, the rally finishes officially at Llanrwst, still some distance from Llandudno. At this 'official' finish there is a service area where cars can be fettled and cleaned before they return to Llandudno. Once in Llandudno, the car should be put on its trailer as quickly as possible, with the service van coupled up. After a day of rallying, service crews and competitors are usually in need of sustenance, generally of the liquid kind! So, get all the real work out of the way first, then you can relax and let your hair down.

As a co-driver, you should check what results are available as soon as you arrive, submitting a 'query form' if and when necessary. You should also establish a rough time for the provisional results to be announced. In this case it is about 21.30, so until then you and the others can disappear to have a meal and freshen up. Once announced as provisional, the results will become final after 30 minutes providing there are no protests. If you have won an award, out of courtesy you should attend the prize presentation, but even if you have not won, it is regarded as good manners to attend. Besides, the bars at rally HQ generally don't close until the early hours of the next morning!

8

Advanced Co-driving

Experience is the keyword for advanced co-driving. No matter how many rallies you have tackled, there is always something waiting round the next corner to catch you out. Although, as the word itself suggests, there is no way you can plan for the unexpected, there are ways which narrow the chances of the unexpected cropping up. Call it 'rallymanship', as Stuart Turner once did, or let it be known as tricks of the trade; these are the unwritten rules of rallying – rules which can never be found in any book of regulations, nor defined by organizers. Good rallies guard themselves against these tricks, whilst top co-drivers employ them to test the unwary.

Basic co-driving will have given you the fundamentals of office management, now it is time to expand into small team management, but most important of all, to learn how to help your driver during special stages. At this level you will be contesting one of the major National-status championships, probably having to look after not just your driver, but at least two mechanics as well. They will all be expecting you to organize everything – particularly, to be staying at the hotel where all the pretty girls are to be found! Your choice of championship is fairly wide-ranging; you will be able to pick a completely forest stage series, a tarmac rally championship, or the RAC National Championship, which contains both forest and tarmac events.

Your job, as always, starts with planning a season's programme for your driver. Whichever championship is chosen, it will have in the region of nine qualifying rounds scattered around the country. Once settled on a series, it is never a bad idea to look for additional smaller rallies which are likely to cover the same stages as the championship rallies. If you have not rallied in a particular area before, then a 'clubbie' event can give a useful insight into the character of forests which a bigger event would use,

but it's no good if the smaller rally is more than two months before your championship rally, unless both you and your driver are blessed with the talent of indelibly remembering forest roads.

Practising over Forestry Commission roads is outlawed, but some of the tarmac rallies do allow competitors to familiarize themselves with the stages and make pacenotes. The technique of pacenoting is dealt with in its own chapter later in the book. For the majority of rallies, the driver will be driving 'blind', so the more information you can relay to him the better. In its infinite wisdom, the RAC MSA once banned the use of OS 1:50 000 maps on all stage rallies except its own World Championship RAC Rally. Then, as mentioned earlier, co-drivers won back the right to use maps, but there were impositions – only road sections and the entry to and exit from forests are allowed to be marked on the maps, and hazards, such as tricky bends or firebreaks, cannot be marked either. To be able to follow a stage route through a forest is still a pretty stiff task, but there is a way of remembering this valued information without breaking the RAC law.

It is only outlawed if marked maps are carried in the competing car; there is nothing stopping them being kept in the service barge for reference at each service halt. The top co-drivers in the country had enough presence of mind to keep master sets of maps from the days when marking was allowed. There are only a few hazards on each stage as a rule, so it isn't too difficult to remember where they are after a quick scan of your 'proper' map at service.

Simple map references on a route card are normally left behind at 'clubbie' level – from now on it is a matter of road books, right through to World Championship Internationals. The majority of events will give Tulip diagram details of each special stage, together with mileages in the road book issued

You have to be prepared to put up with an awful lot as a co-driver! Arne Hertz tried to counterbalance Hannu Mikkola's Audi Quattro on the 1983 Lombard RAC Rally after the front suspension broke. (*Bishop*)

at signing-on. But organizers of higher-grade rallies issue the stage route printed on the reverse of the individual stage time cards which are handed to co-drivers on the startline of each stage – now that's a problem which cannot be overcome in predicting accurately the intended roads to be used! It calls for immediate awareness and pretty nifty navigational map work. Luckily, this is not the case in by far the majority of events, so it is possible to mark up a set of master maps with the entire rally route even before you start.

Ordnance Survey maps, however, do not show every single forestry road, so don't be surprised if your route peters out in the middle of a vast expanse of green. It is then time to try tracing the stage route back through the forest from the finish – just remember to beware of the void in the middle, though, for as sure as eggs is eggs, that's where the tricky bits are!

To help in reading maps, a magnifier should be used, just as in road rallies, but it may need modifying for use in daylight. An ordinary magnifier is fine for night use with its low-wattage bulb; in daylight, however, the ambient light will probably be more than the bulb produces – and it will still appear dark inside the magnifier. You could try fitting a more powerful bulb, but that will more than likely mean a new lampholder and there may not be enough room to fit it inside the casing. Some magnifiers with part of the casing cut away allow enough light to be shed on the map, but it is no good using a magnifier unless it makes the job of reading a map easier.

If you have transferred all of the route on to maps, make absolutely sure you have marked the position of passage controls and card collection points as well. They can easily be missed, even if you are using the road book itself, so it is useful to mark them with a flourescent marker pen, just as it is to mark any important instruction. Picked out in such a way on the page narrows the chances of sailing straight past them on the road.

Get yourself well organized before the start with maps stowed away in the correct order of use and the road book ready at the right page. You will have more time cards than on a road rally, and you will be expected to hand them in at card collection points, which are usually passage controls as well. It is your job to transfer the last time from one card on to the next card. Although you only need one card at a time, keep them all together on a clipboard – it sounds simple, but if you lose one, you are out of the rally!

Sometimes, things tend to get hectic at stage finishes and you may not have time to record your stage time on a record sheet, so it is best to just scribble it down in the road book, then transfer it properly later. Some organizers make your work easier by printing a check sheet in the back of the road book, but it is a good idea to keep your own book of record sheets anyway. Keep records of other crews' times as well; this is the only way you can be sure of your overall position in the rally at any one point, and they obviously help in checking results at the finish. If you cannot find times for a certain competitor – perhaps he is running too far in front or behind to check times whilst waiting at stage starts –

try finding the *Motoring News* or *Autosport* man, who will probably be keeping his own record anyway. That way it also gives you a chance of telling him how your are fairing, or giving excuses for not being in the lead!

At service areas, when wandering around checking stage times with other co-drivers, always be aware of their problems. If their team is the centre of frenzied activity it is a fair assumption they have a problem – and problems can lead to retirement if they worsen. Maybe exerting a little more pressure on stages would see that team's retirement. Check, too, whether a rival has enough new tyres, as part-worn rubber will tend to give less grip. When your car has new tyres fitted and there is a lengthy road section following, it is not good strategy to drive too fast and scrub valuable rubber from the tread. Tyres are the most important link with performance on forest roads and regular changes should be planned, but remember that a different size of tyre will affect your tripmeter calibration.

There could be a series of stages within one forest complex where no servicing of cars is allowed. In this

'We can see you!' No, it's not a device to help team manager Tony Fall keep an even closer eye on his drivers; camera work is just one of the things a top team has to entertain. Walter Röhrl puts the Ascona through its paces on the 1982 Tour of Corsica Rally.

The co-driver's compartment of a factory Audi Quattro. To the right is the purposeful Halda computer tripmeter and time recorder, with a pair of accurate timepieces bolted to the top of the dashboard. On top of the dashboard a spare map light bulb and fuses are taped safely in place, whilst underneath are the control boxes for the car's ignition system, together with a battery cut-off switch. (*Bishop*)

Co-drivers Bjorn Cederberg (foreground) and Mike Greasley check each other's stage times at a short service halt on the 1983 Lombard RAC Rally. Keeping constant tabs on the opposition is essential. (*Bishop*)

'Where did you say the road went?' In snow, it is a definite disadvantage to run as first car on the road; just imagine trying to sort this lot out with no wheel tracks to follow! (*Bishop*)

case, there is no reason why you shouldn't carry two spare wheels in the car and change on to the fresh rubber (the driving wheels only) when the old tyres have lost their grip – as long as work is carried out by the driver and co-driver using spares and tools carried in the rally car. Repairs can similarly be made to the car, but there is generally a restriction on the type of work permitted inside a control area.

Once you have arrived at the special stage and cleared the Stage Arrival control, you may have to queue to start the actual special stage (if there was a queue, even at the arrival control, you should have got out, walked to the marshal and booked in on time – it was not your fault you couldn't get the car into the control area). If you have been delayed on the road for any reason, you should ask the crews in front if you can jump the queue back into your proper position, but if they refuse, don't argue; they are in the right, not you!

As a rule of thumb, it is better to let as few cars as possible take a run at a stage before you. The roads will have deteriorated more with the passage of each car; you should therefore take advantage of the

target timing system with its 'dead time' between Stage Arrival and Stage Start – jumping the queue will not be penalized, but you won't be the most popular crew in the rally! However, a less aggravating way of climbing the running order is to simply be ready to cash in on others' misfortunes. If the car in front is having difficulty in firing up, nip past him and take the next available stage start time.

Some forests are notorious for giving a definite advantage to the first car on the road, like the stages within the Kielder complex on the Scottish border. There, crews will jostle for early positions in the running order. The same applies in the summertime, or when there has been a long dry spell before the rally, leaving the stages in a dusty condition. If it is a still day (or night), the dust will hang in the air for more than a minute, meaning the car following is always driving in fog-like conditions. Running first car on the stage will pay dividends, but if it is not possible, you should be prepared to employ delaying tactics to allow more than a minute between you and the car in front. The bigger the gap you have, the more time there is for the dust to settle.

Organizers, however, are well aware of such delaying manoeuvres as they will soon stretch the event over a longer time span. On the other hand, some organizers have the sense to plan for this and start cars at two-minute intervals anyway. Pressure can be put on the stage start officials to allow you an extra minute gap for simple safety reasons – there is always more dust in the air around the braking area for a bend, and that is just where you most need good visibility! If pleas look like failing, you could always try puncturing a tyre on purpose (although that is a pretty drastic measure); or make hard work of cranking your car engine to delay your starting the stage. If the arrival control is out of sight of the stage start, then simply crawling between the two could have the desired result, but remember the rules in this case are always on the side of the officials; if they say start a stage at a certain time and you don't, there will be a penalty to pay!

On the other hand, if the stages are covered in snow, the first car has a disadvantage. There will generally be tyre tracks on the forest roads, put there by marshals' cars and course vehicles, but in 'white out' conditions, the more marks on the road the better. You should aim to delay your start time, but unlike the case in dusty conditions, you are not looking for just a bigger gap between cars, you are looking instead for more cars to tackle the stage before you. In top-class championship rallying this will lead to cat-and-mouse games between stages, with crews hiding up side roads, just off route, to allow a rival to pass unwittingly and having to tackle the stage as first car!

At the start of every special stage, check the time the car in front leaves the actual start line – he may jump the start or be given a helping few seconds from a 'friendly' marshal. It is always more advantageous to have 'friends' at the stage finish! If he does jump the start and the marshals do not seem unduly bothered, you should point out the error. If they still seem unperturbed, make sure you jump the start by more than the car in front. Finns are particularly good at that, especially in Finland, where the words 'three, two and one' in Finnish all sound remarkably similar.

On the stages themselves, be on the lookout for groups of spectators, especially along stretches of straight roads – they are there to see something happen! It could indicate a jump or a hidden chicane-type bend. Collecting a rally programme at the start will show where all spectator points are, and they can be marked on the set on maps kept in the service car which you refer to for 'dodgy bits'. If you find some unexpected spectators, approach with caution! You should also be on the lookout for missing arrows, particularly where they should form a 'gate' to pass through. If one has been knocked

down, it may allow you to short-cut a corner, but on no account should you deliberately drive 'behind' a standing arrow – you are technically not following the correct stage route and face a penalty of exclusion if you are spotted by a Judge of Fact.

On long special stages, your driver will probably need more encouragement than on shorter ones. His concentration will need to be kept sharp and you should tell him how far away the finish is, but don't tell him the actual distance unless he asks for it. Drivers can very rarely equate distances when driving flat-out through a forest, so it is much better to just tell him when you reach quarter-distance, half-distance, and so on. But you should be very aware of the exact distance to the finish, for it is on long stages where punctures can play a crucial part in the end result.

A well-practised wheel change should take just over two minutes, depending on what type of jack is being used. If you were to stop mid-stage to change wheels, that time loss has to be weighed up against the distance left to the stage finish and your increase in stage time due to the handicap of a flat tyre. You also have to bear in mind the long-term damage to the car in running on a damaged tyre. If will start off as a simple flat, then the tyre will either roll off the rim completely or disintegrate steadily. When it rolls off, leaving you with a solid wheel in contact with the road, wheel bearings and half-shafts can be damaged due to the lack of cushioning effect of the tyre. If it were to disintegrate, there is a chance that wire within the tyre casing will become tangled up in other vital mechanicals of the car and the flailing rubber will undoubtedly damage any lightweight wheelarches fitted to the car.

There are no hard and fixed rules about punctures, but it is fair to say a flat can be driven on for about a mile with little danger, but after a couple of miles it will start either breaking up or rolling off the wheel rim – the less twisty the stage, then obviously the longer it will stay in one piece. You should also bear in mind whether or not there is service directly after the stage, where mechanical damage could be repaired. On tarmac stages, of course, the situation is less critical with regard to mechanical damage, but stage times will increase drastically by running on a flat racing tyre.

If you decide to stop and change the wheel, leaving one wheel nut off can save time without danger – but put the nut in your pocket, and remember everything will be very hot if you have already driven for over a mile on the stage. If your spare and jack are in the boot, and there are no vital components to be damaged, leave the old wheel and jack loose to save time. If, however, they are carried inside the car, make sure they are all secured before you start off again – and remember to fasten your

Practising a wheel change can shave minutes off the time it will take in a forest stage with other cars flashing past all the time. Sensibly, this crew has picked some solid ground on which to stop, so the jack won't sink. (*Large*)

seat belts! If you are lost in the road book or on the map after changing a wheel (or after a stop for any other reason) tell your driver he is on his own until you find your place again.

It is possible you could catch a slower car on a long stage, and tell-tale plumes of dust in the air on bends are the things to look for. As soon as you see the car, your driver should switch on his headlights and, when close enough, start using the car's horn to let the crew in front know you are behind and want to pass. It is quite possible for a driver to press on completely unaware of a car catching him, so if he doesn't pull over straight away don't hold it against him, but if he delays you for over half a mile a word in his ear is called for at the stage finish. When you catch a car, don't close right up behind it as flying stones will certainly damage the front of your car. When you overtake, your driver similarly should not use full power until well clear of the slower car. On night stages this is particularly important as driving lights are especially vulnerable to flying stones. If you do power straight past a slower car and break the

other driver's lights, you can expect a visit from him at the next service area – probably with a wheelbrace in his hand!

When preparing the rally car, it is useful to duplicate important controls on your side of the car, such as horn button, wiper and washer switches, and perhaps even fuse boxes and relays. The horn is handy for you to use if you are first car on the road to warn spectators walking on the stage, but it should be used sparingly unless you want to look like a right *prima donna*. Wipers and washers could be vital for you to control when coming across some water unexpectedly – the driver will undoubtedly be too busy trying to regain control of the car to bother with finding the wiper switch!

In the unlikely event of your car leaving the road, you should firstly check to see if you can get it back on to the road, perhaps with the help of spectators. Then you should remember that there is another car behind, which could do the same! Leave your driver to sort things out, whilst you run back up the road to warn the next and subsequent cars of the hazard. If it

Whatever you do, don't emulate this foolish co-driver. Windows should be either closed, or open just an inch. Never tackle a stage with your hand out of the window like this. Accidents tend to happen quickly and unexpectedly. If this car rolled, the co-driver would probably lose his fingers. (*Bishop*)

Part of the art of advanced co-driving is knowing who not to sit next to. This chap is obviously proud of his past indiscretions, but I wonder if his co-drivers share his feelings? (*Bishop*)

is just a passing visit to a ditch, it is unfortunately the co-driver's job to get out and push!

In addition to stepping up the level of help you can give to a driver, you will have to be managing a team as well. You will have service crews wanting to know where to go and what time to be there, as well as how long the rally car can be worked on. The best method of planning is by drawing up a service schedule. It should indicate the location of service points, along with a designation letter or number. Any expected work, such as changing to a certain type of tyre and the amount of fuel to be taken on, should also be shown. The service crew should be given enough time to travel from one point to another, together with a map showing their best route. The planning of a schedule at National Championship level is fairly easy as servicing is greatly restricted to permitted areas only, generally sited between two service (SV) controls with a specific time allowance given between the 'In' and 'Out' controls.

When you arrive at a service area, you should give instructions (you call them instructions, the service crew calls them requests!) to just one mechanic as to what work is needed, with the understanding that the rest of the team ask him what needs doing. He is the man you keep updating on the time situation and it is generally a good idea to keep a few minutes in hand, just in case there is congestion at the 'Out' control. If a major repair job is called for and time is running short, you should go to the control and wait for your driver there. Theoretically, the marshal should only give you a time through the control when the car and crew is inside the control area, but a bit of smooth talking may see them accepting your excuse and booking you in on time, even though your car still has no rear axle fitted! Biding your time until the moment of most confusion could pay dividends here, as an inexperienced marshal will undoubtedly crack under pressure.

The service schedule can only be planned when the road book is available, which on Nationals will be at signing-on. However, it will be useful to write a movement schedule for the team as soon as the Final Instructions arrive. It will already have been your job to arrange the entry for the rally and book the necessary hotels. From that information, a basic movement plan can be drawn, detailing where any one team member should be at any given time, but also detailing free time. It should contain details of how to find the start and what time to be there; where scrutineering and noise check are sited; where the Rally HQ is located; where the team hotel is and possibly the whereabouts of a local garage stocking parts for your particular car, together with the manager's name and telephone number. It should also be agreed that in the event of any problems, a key team member can be contacted, or a message left for him.

Service crews should also be issued with their expenses money (if any!) and told to collect receipts for everything they purchase. Fuel cans should be filled before the rally start and all tyres checked for pressure. The rally car should be fitted with the correct tyres for the first stages and be fuelled with the right amount of petrol before the start – although this will only be known after a service schedule has been drawn up. Each service barge should also have a check list of items to be loaded and, if they are used on an event, they should, of course, be replaced before the next outing.

A co-driver's last job before the start is to make sure all the necessary stickers are in place on the car and that all the paperwork is in order. Then, if time permits, get some sleep!

At the rally finish, all your own stage times and those of rivals should be checked off against your own records. Any errors (not in your favour) should be pointed out to the organizers by way of a 'query', not a protest. Only as a last resort should a protest be made – as with road rallies, some teams make it their policy never to protest, even when they are obviously right to do so. Protests do tend to leave a nasty taste in everyone's mouth and therefore should be steered clear of if at all possible.

Finally, when everything is over, you should make sure not to leave any unpaid bills behind, including those promised pints to spectators who dragged your car from the ditch after your driver's brainstorm. To round everything off, send copies of the results to all the team members, not forgetting to write and let any sponsors know of the outcome and supplying them with press cuttings as well. It is not a bad idea, either, to keep your local press and radio stations informed of your driver's progress through the year.

9

Pacenotes

Way back in road rallying, the navigator's job was to read information from maps to help the driver. A little foresight in knowing what to expect around the next corner always helped. As you progressed through road rallies, you built up a massive library of information with markings. Those markings were outlawed in the forests, but the co-driver (if also a navigator) still helped by reading just what the Ordnance Survey had marked on its own maps. However, that information could be so inaccurate it showed just how ineffectual the maps were for maximum performance – they simply showed the obvious hazard or sharp bend. There was a definite need for some other aid, and the answer lay in pacenotes – a written description of roads, usually recorded in a unique type of shorthand which, to the unitiated, resembled ancient hieroglyphics.

The system of noting was really started back in the 1950s and can be credited to Denis Jenkinson, who partnered Stirling Moss to that marvellous Mille Miglia win in 1955. Then, 'Jenks' wrote route notes on a roll of paper strapped to his leg and gave Moss the required foresight to see around the next corner. The notes were soon accepted in rallying and have since become accepted as the norm in all but a few countries – Britain, unfortunately, being one of those few countries! Making and reading pacenotes is the pinnacle of rally co-driving – so, if the World Championship is your goal, start reading here. . .

World Championship events use them on every round except the Lombard RAC Rally and they are found in almost every foreign International and National across the world. Only four countries involved in top-flight rallying abstain – Finland, Sweden, the USA and Britain – and even then there are exceptions. Finland allows notes on its World Championship Rally of the 1000 Lakes and Arctic Rally, while some tarmac rallies on the Isle of Man,

in Northern Ireland and over the Eppynt ranges in Wales allow the only use in mainland Britain. Most of our rallying uses Forestry Commission roads and the overlords there do not want cars whizzing around the forests making notes when normal work is being carried out – mind you, I doubt if rally crews would appreciate meeting a 30-tonne forestry truck around a blind corner, either! Tarmac rallies in Britain and Ireland are slightly different. The Isle of Man has long since allowed pacenotes, as have the organizers of rallies on Eppynt. Now, Ulster and even Southern Ireland are starting to allow their use; however, there are restrictions on cars to be used for recces and strict speed limits are imposed – and policed strongly.

Find a deserted stretch of road and time yourself over it at night, reading the road from a map, then drive over it again slowly, making written notes instead. You will find your description of the corners is more accurate and you will be able to spot brows or crests in the road which a map can rarely show. Then retime yourself, using the notes instead of the map – you will see the difference. Now translate that into your performance over a complete rally – the advantage is quite plain to see!

The transfer of map information into words is not really true pacenoting, it is more a safety note system, just describing exactly what is ahead on the road. Safety notes are alright in some respects, but still do not give the opportunity for maximum speed over roads. If time is short in making proper notes, they are fine and some of the commercially available notes for places like Eppynt or sections of the Manx rallies are a refined version of safety notes.

Pacenotes should be unique to the driver, *not* the co-driver, and he calls the shots. So what's this doing in a book on co-driving? Well, although notes are made by the driver, the co-driver acts as the

Pacenotes are the ultimate aid in navigation and World Championship co-drivers pride themselves on the notes they produce. Good sets of notes should be concise, neat and well-presented, just like these, which were prepared for Ari Vatanen. (*Bishop*)

prompter in reading them back, and there is a real knack to it. These are a furtherance of map markings and so an extension of safety notes. They tell the driver which corners can be driven faster than they look, instead of which are slower than they look.

Details of special stage routes on 'practice' events will be issued in advance of the rally, ranging from over a month to just a day, depending on the individual event. The co-driver's first task is to plan a schedule for pacenoting, instead of just blindly driving around the whole route as it is laid out by the organizers. By splitting the route up into groups of stages close to each other, it will be possible to cover the entire event quicker. But, make sure you drive each road section at least once as well, and time exactly how long it takes to cover it driving sensibly. This way, if you have to stop for repairs during the rally, you know exactly how long that road section should take to complete. You should also note any possible situations which could delay you, such as road works or passing through factory areas at going-home time – and you should also bear in mind that there will be spectators on the actual rally, who

can cause unpredictable hold-ups.

When pacenoting the stages themselves, you will find that the rally organizers have somehow marked the route on the road – whether by painting the position and direction of stage arrows on the road surface, or placing boards at junctions indicating which way to turn. There is no excuse for not knowing exactly where you are all the time. Before starting out on a day's recceing, always check the Official Noticeboard at Rally HQ for any route changes or amendments. Also, if a certain stage is used in both directions, organizers often impose a one-way system of recceing, *i.e.* one direction during the morning and the reverse direction in the afternoon – it helps ease the situation, for although pacenoting should be carried out at low speeds, some roads are only wide enough for one car and the resultant jam from two-way traffic can waste a whole morning.

You should let the driver 'read' everything to you, making rough notes in pencil in your book as he does so. A ring-bound notebook is probably the best to use, but it is all down to personal choice – after a few events you will soon decide for yourself. You may find it useful to drive stages at least three or four times, but if time is tight, take your time on the first run and make neat pacenotes from the word go, then always drive each stage once again to check them.

If you make rough notes in pencil first, it allows you to rub out mistakes or alter them easily, but when transferring them to a neat copy book later, be sure to go out and check them over the stages again – it has been known for entire lines to be missed out! Make no mistake, rewriting notes takes up an awful lot of a co-driver's time before rallies – time which your driver generally spends socializing!

Notes tell a driver exactly what to do – it's a bit like a computer programme. Even an experienced driver will take time to build consistency into his notes on each event and, above all, it's that consistency which is important. It doesn't matter if a fast right is called a 'looney' right as long as the driver can relate to it. The same applies to distances; just as in reading roads from a map, they may not bear any resemblance to actual distances, but they should be kept consistent. Above all, descriptions should be concise; make no mistake, when a driver is pulling 9,000 in fourth or fifth, bends come up bloody quickly! Use single-syllable words whenever possible and grade corners in as few different categories as possible.

By far the best way of introducing yourself to notes is to borrow someone else's and check them against the actual road by driving them. The first difference you will notice between pacenotes and safety notes (or map reading), is how much 'faster' the corners are designated. On a road rally, your '45 right' could well be described as a 'fast right', whilst a 'square 90 right' could be a 'slow right'. By looking through an example of some top driver's notes you will soon get the idea.

Two methods of pacenoting have come to the fore over the years. One is to grade roads by description in abbreviated words, and the other is to number them, the numbers increasing with the severity of the corner.

The abbreviated word method generally starts with 'absolute' as the fastest, almost imperceptible, corner and moves on through 'fast', 'medium' and 'K' to 'slow' and 'hairpin'. The number system may possibly be more adaptable, but is not yet as widely used. Flat-out corners are graded as '1', whilst '6' or '7' could be a 'square 90'. There is no real ceiling to the system, but it is doubtful whether a '9 right' could be taken any faster than a '13 right'! In either system you may have to regrade certain fast corners as you progress through noting the stages and it is easily done by prefixing them with 'very' to give further detail. Some drivers also include a number to indicate where the apex of the corner is: '1' would be an early apex, '3' a late apex. Some continentals,

R̊ (°°)	Absolute right	C	Crest
Ŗ	Flat right	/c	Over crest
VFR	Very fast right	gt	Gate
FR	Fast right	gd	Grid
MR	Medium right	↑	Climbs
KR	'K' right	↓	Drops
SR	Slow right	!	Care
HPR	Hairpin right		
		→	Into
Lg	Long	+	And
VLg	Very long	50·100	50m, 100m, etc...
<	Opens	⌂	Building
>	Narrows	🌲	Tree
?	Maybe	⬆	Road sign

Abbreviations really speak for themselves, but here are a few standard notations. An absolute is the fastest corner and a hairpin the slowest. Extra information can be given to describe them as long, opens, tightens (narrows), or maybe when a corner could be faster than it appears. Groups of notes to be read out together should be linked by underlining or placing inside brackets, and a co-driver could add his own notes referring to landmarks in a different colour to indicate they are just to jog his memory, not for reading out.

SS.1   BRANDYWELL 1   10.98 Kms

STAGE STARTS JUST AFTER GRID

LgR̊ 70 VFR + SL 200

VFL 70 SL 70 VFL 20

LgFL 150 SR 200 R̊ 200

FL + VFL< 200

VFR BRIDGE to LgFR 150

FL< 250 VFL/GRID 70

L̊ 100 POST FR 250

VFL + R̊ 200 C.MR 50

L̊ 50 SR 20 POST FL 20

L̊ 50 ML + FR 20 ⟶

Above is an example of commercially available 'safety notes' produced by Terry Harryman for the Manx International. Compare them to the notes (below), which he used when co-driving Ari Vatanen over the same section of road, and see how much 'faster' they become.

BRANDYWELL

R̈̊ 70 ER? 20 L̊?

200 >EL 100 L̊

100 L̊? 70 L OK

200 R̊ 300 R̊

200 L̊? 70 L̊? Ⓢ

< 300 R̊? 50 LgR

E = easy   Ⓢ = stay in

particularly the French, grade corners by the gear in which to take them, but the problem with this system is that a fourth-gear bend on a dry road could become a third-gear corner when wet.

Pacenotes are really an idiot's guide to driving because they not only detail exactly what the road does, they actually tell the driver what to do. Compared with reading a map, or safety notes, a series of bends will change dramatically when described in pacenotes. Take, for example, a section of road which on the ground looks like this: 200 metres to a 20-degree left-hander, a further 20 metres to a tight 90-degree left-hander, then 20 metres to an open 90-degree right-hander and on to a straight for 200 metres. Map reading or safety notes would read: '200 – 20 left (or flat left) – 20 – 90 left – 20 – open 90 right – 200'. Pacenotes, however, could read: '200 – left tightens to slow left into flat

right 200'.

The '90-degree right' changes to 'flat right' because the car is travelling slowly enough around the previous 90-degree left-hander to accelerate all the way round the right; and the '200' tagged on to the end of the note lets the driver know he can keep 'the pedal to the metal' out of the corner as well – or at least he has enough distance between the last and next corners to sort out the mess he's got himself into!

Reading notes is almost an art, but a good grounding in road rallying should tell a co-driver how to time each instruction. If bends are grouped together, they should be read like that, but always give a driver advance warning of sharp bends when you are travelling through fast corners. Instructions should always end with the distance to the next corner or instruction; that way a driver knows how to

These are Hannu Mikkola's notes for the Monte Carlo Rally, produced by Arne Hertz. They are still in their rough form, ready for alterations to be made. Each driver has his own method of noting; the main differences here are the use of a minus (L–) to indicate a tight 90-degree bend and 'S' to indicate a slight bend. Mikkola does not use 'F' for fast, instead using 'S' for slight. Flat is shown as 'f1' and absolute as 'A'.

pace himself through the present bend. The way in which notes are written down helps here, too. As a rule of thumb, distances less than 50 metres should not be called; it is better to use 'into' when one corner blends into another, then use 'and' when there is a short straight in between.

Some co-drivers write notes continuously across the page of a notebook, grouping instructions together by underlining them, but the best method is to use a separate line for each group of instructions; unfortunately, it means you could resemble Moses with his tablets of stone having to lug around so many books. Some continental co-drivers write notes up a page instead of across. Again, there are so many different methods that it's best to look around, try each one, then settle for the one which suits you best, but writing across a page is by far the most popular and you would be advised to adopt this

method just in case you need to borrow someone else's notes at any time.

Even the best co-drivers can lose their place in the notes, so it is advisable to build in little reminders. Junctions may not be obvious when reading notes – a driver does not need to know that a 'K right' is also a junction as he will be driving as if in blinkers. Simply marking a 'J' (say in red) in your notes helps as a landmark for you. Similarly, you can mark other landmarks for your own information – try putting them inside brackets to indicate they are not to be read out to the driver, but just used as a reference.

At the top of each page, write the name of the stage and the page number of notes for that particular stage, together with the total number of pages *i.e.* Brandywell 1 of 6. Then write in the number of the next sheet at the bottom of each page – this helps in spotting if you have inadvertently

Mike Broad's notes, here, for Russell Brookes on a desert rally show each instruction on a new line. It is not usually advisable to use movable items like oil drums or boxes as reference points, but in the desert, anything goes . . . even including that rare commodity known as grass!

RAS-AL-BAR
BAHRAIN INT. RALLY.

NOTES. R. BROOKES ①

R 600

L + R   300

VVlgL KeepL 600

Care Washaways. Box (R?)
HEAD FOR CONE.

PASSAGE CONTROL AT
RED FLAG

Look For PASSAGE CONTROL OHPR.

FORK R OF RED FLAG . (Zero Trip) (1·5)

Follow track 1·5km   Keep R of 1st Junction .

L opposite Oil Drum on RIGHT (P/Control?)
(Zero Trip)(2·7km)

Right by Grass on Right .

turned over two pages. You could also use a colour code, which is easier to spot than a written number. When you are on the stage, the speed with which everything happens is incredibly fast and your mind will be almost totally occupied (save for a modicum of brain space reserved for thoughts of self preservation!), so you should be aiming to make life extremely simple for yourself. If you mark, say, a red spot at the bottom of a page and a similar red spot appears at the top of the continuation page everything is OK – if, however, the spot is, for example, blue then you've turned over to the wrong page.

Your notebook page should be about A5, which is about half the size of an A4 sheet of paper, and it should never be written to entirely fill the width of the page – enough room (about an inch and a half) should be left as a margin on either side to allow you to hold the book securely in both hands without obscuring an instruction. Although notes written in a thick black pencil are adequate, you should aim to produce a set of notes using a good black felt-tip pen – but make sure it's waterproof; 'Sod's Law' dictates they will get covered in water at some point during the rally! Stages should be noted in the book in the order in which they are to be used on the rally, with any duplicated stages referred back to, or photocopied and inserted in the correct place. However, you may even change a note during the rally, so remember to transfer the correction to any duplicated sheets as well.

Night-time stages are best noted at night, when all the little brows and crests that are unseen in daylight will soon show up in a car's lights. Landmarks could also be lost in the darkness, whilst others, such as reflective signs, may be more prevalent. As far as possible, stages should be driven over at the same time of day as the rally is to use them – you must always aim to reproduce rally conditions as closely as possible. A corner driven in the early morning could cause the driver to be blinded by a low dazzling sun, whereas in the afternoon it could be in deep shadow. Any severe changes in conditions need to be noted. Changes of surface are the obvious ones, but roads driven in the dry could turn lethal when wet. Patches of slick tarmac are fine in the dry, but like ice during rain, and depressions in the road edges could collect water and form large aquaplane-producing puddles. Gravel is another hazard on tarmac rallies – and it takes a surprisingly little amount of the stuff to send a racing-tyred car spinning off into the scenery at high speed if a wheel lands on it. Kerbstones should also be remembered. On the rally itself, there are bound to be spectators gathering on corners and junctions, so landmarks could be obscured, as could route direction arrows – and caution boards. Pacenotes should not stop at the flying finish board (the rally car doesn't stop there, so why should the notes?) – so continue making (and reading) notes until you reach the 'Stop' control. If you are not partnering your regular driver, ask if you can take a copy of his notes after the rally – remember that

Top crews very often use rally car replicas to carry out pacenoting and for practising. Timo Salonen and Seppo Harjanne are seen here using an old Datsun Violet to recce the Monte. (*Bishop*)

notes are the driver's property, not yours.

Whenever possible, you should practise the stages at almost rally speeds as well, although this applies to foreign rallies as there are generally (and rightly, too) strict speed restrictions imposed on British pacenoted events. On the Continent, top crews will regularly have a spare replica rally car for practising, along with a service crew as well, but the number of accidents which occur during this high-speed practising are numerous. By using other team members with radios, it is possible to almost seal off a public road used as a stage for 'illegal' high-speed practice. From a competitor's point of view, though, this is a very advisable pastime. Small bumps on corners could pass unnoticed during low-speed recceing, but on the rally they can throw a car completely off line, resulting in a pretty hairy accident – make no mistake, that occurs quite often as even the most experienced driver can miss such a hazard. But high-speed practice has to be weighed up against the public image of rallies using closed public roads as special stages. Every maimed moggie or frightened Fido will bring countless complaints against the sport and jeopardize the whole future of road usage.

Pacenoting on anything other than tarmac rallies is more difficult as there are many more factors involved. Rocks can appear in the middle of the road, kicked up by the car in front, or unsurfaced roads can be washed away after heavy rainfall – these notes, I feel, fall into the category of a mixture of safety/pacenotes, not pure pacenotes. Where dust can be expected (or fog or mist on tarmac rallies) it is a good idea to include trip distances in your notes. On many rallies they are essential, where stage distances run into tens of kilometres over featureless countryside.

There are variations on the pacenote theme as well, but they are restricted to specialized events. On rallies where temperatures can vary continuously and rapidly with changes of altitude, wet roads can become icy or icy roads become wet. Ice note crews are used on the Monte Carlo Rally, sent into stages before the rally passes through to mark up copies of a crew's notes with any changes, such as extra ice. Different crews have different methods, but they all

Test No.	Name / Col	Crew	Test Start	Car at S.P.	Your next test	Approx distance to your next test	Notes	page 6
10	Porte/St. Roch 16 km (also Test 34 Crew A)	C	10.09 Mon	09.40 Mon	11	30 km	Look for rocks and icy patches in shade. Do not get caught at finish with road closed. No easy return, except over Turini. Drive Turini in daytime then rest at Hotel Trois Vallees, Turini.	
11	Turini 22 km (also Test 26 Crew C)	C	07.00 Tues	06.20 Tues	14	240 km	They close Turini earlier each year! It is important that you are driving the test from midnight onwards. Drive inside test until police close it. Note most carefully any ice on early part & snow put on road by spectators. Then stay at top until latest time before driving to S.P. Long drive round to S.P. Don't be late!	
12	Miolans/St Auban 24 km (also Test 28 Crew A)	A	08.57	08.00	16	220 km	A critical test – take care over thawing & freezing in sun & shade, also fallen rocks. After test, call at Gap to compare notes and rest at Hotel de la Paix.	
13	Faye 12 km	B	12.08	11.40	17	150 km	After test, call at Gap to compare notes & rest at Hotel de la Paix.	
14	Espreaux 32 km	C	12.58	12.30	18	220 km (150 km to Novotel)	After test, call at Gap to compare notes. Then proceed Novotel, Valence to rest before driving (18) St Bonnet.	

Ice note crews are used on the Monte Carlo Rally to check the conditions of stages just before the rally passes through. Careful planning has to go into producing a schedule for ice noting, like this example produced by Phil Short for the Audi team.

usually centre on underlining in a variety of colours to indicate either ice or water. A similar thing occurs on tropical rallies, such as the Safari, where crews (mud note crews this time) are sent to investigate suspect patches of road where rain could turn a dusty track into a tenacious quagmire.

Until the day British crews are given the right to pacenote roads, we shall all have to turn to Europe for the experience. But if a rally organizer gives you the chance of recceing a route – take that opportunity and use it to your utmost advantage! As you will have found from earlier chapters, prior knowledge is your greatest ally in rallying.

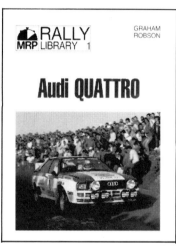

10

Internationals at Home

Moving on into the world of International rallies is moving on into the world of professionals. Where rules and regulations were previously a little lax, now they are strictly enforced to cope with the skill and ingenuity of the professional teams. The best teams employ the best brains, there to exploit to the full any loopholes an inexperienced organizer may leave open. In Britain, International rallies are still organized by amateurs; even the Lombard RAC Rally cannot keep an organizer employed full-time. But organizers have a myriad rules and regulations on their side, and extra officials, sometimes from overseas, help to control the events.

International rallying in Britain is not simply governed by the RAC Motor Sport Association, just as foreign events are not solely the responsibility of that particular country's sporting governing body (ASN). International rallies can be entered by anyone holding a recognized International Competition Licence issued by their home ASN. Because of this, competitors look towards a central body to govern the sport – a central body which can impose the rules to be obeyed by organizers of International rallies anywhere in the world. That body is the *Federation Internationale Automobile* (FIA), base in Paris, which, through the FISA (*Federation Internationale du Sport Automobile*) looks after motor sport, both racing and rallying, worldwide.

The FIA issues its rules in book form annually (coloquially known as the Yellow Book), just as the RAC MSA issues its own Blue Book. The hierarchy of rally regulations has the Yellow Book at its pinnacle, followed in Britain by the RAC Blue Book, then the Regulations for individual events. Luckily, there are few differences between the RAC rules and the FIA rules. For the co-driver, the rules are generally the same, but are enforced a little more enthusiastically. The driver, however, now has to look more closely at his car.

Until this point in the rally spectrum, a car's specification has been relatively free. Any model could be used and modifications to make it more competitive have generally been unrestricted, but not so in the world of Internationals. Cars now have to comply with the vehicle rules of Appendix J in the FIA Yellow Book, and are scrutineered for their eligibility before each rally. At the time of writing, the FIA allows three basic categories of car to compete at International level. These are cars complying with Groups B, A and N.

Group B: Sports cars having a production run of at least 200 identical models within a 12-month period.

Group A: Series production saloons having a production run of at least 5,000 identical models in a 12-month period.

Group N: Series production saloons having a production run of at least 5,000 identical models in a 12-month period.

Cars in Groups B and A can be modified in accordance with strict FIA rules, but cars in Group N are basically in 'showroom' trim only.

It is the responsibility of a particular manufacturer to have its car recognized by the FISA (for FISA championships) for entry in a certain Group. The FISA issues an homologation number to each eligible car after it has been satisfied by the manufacturer in question that the model meets the necessary requirements of production. FISA allows certain modifications under its Groups B and A regulations, so special parts can be offered for competition use – this is known as a process of evolution, but sufficient numbers of these 'evolution models' must be produced by a manufacturer: the minimum order is 10% of the basic production run

'... and I say I haven't had enough yet, Captain!' Stig Blomqvist and 'Captain' Bjorn Cederberg seem to be having a difference of opinion over the spoils of winning the 1983 Lombard RAC Rally. It's always the co-driver who gets the raw deal! (*Large*)

for any Group, with the exception of Group N, whose cars cannot be modified. When a car model has been successfully accepted by the FISA, a set of homologation papers is stamped and sets of these papers must be produced by each rally competitor at scutineering to allow the officials to check that his car complies with the manufacturers' approved competition specification.

In plain language, cars in Group B are the factory team cars which are capable of winning International rallies outright. They have been carefully designed with that sole purpose in mind, and usually result from a massive budget – having to produce 200 base models, then another 20 evolution models is a pretty pricey affair, after which the manufacturer has to try to sell the 200 base models, which, because of their competition-based design, are generally only attractive as road cars to a few hardened enthusiasts. Typical examples of cars in Group B are the Lancia

Rally 037, Audi Sport Quattro, Peugeot 205 Turbo 16 and Renault 5 Turbo.

Cars in Group A are more of a clubman's car and resemble a modified normal production model. They are in rallying to win class positions rather than outright victories, but amongst other cars in the Group, competition is fierce. It is generally the 'clever' manufacturer who wins in Group A: the manufacturer who has carefully thought out a package of modifications at a reasonable cost. Successful cars in this category have been the VW Golf GTI, Toyota Corolla and Alfa Romeo GTV6, although Ford's Escort RS1600i has also seen some success.

Group N cars have still to catch on in Britain, but on the Continent, entire championships revolve around a particular manufacturer's model. Cars such as the Fiat Ritmo 130TC or the Peugeot 205 GTI feature strongly, whilst the Alfa GTV6 has also proved itself an excellent Group N car on tarmac rallies. In Britain, where the majority of rallying is on gravel forest roads, the cars are more likely to break their unstrengthened components than on a tarmac rally, which has probably been the deciding factor in convincing many would-be Group N drivers to give the idea a miss.

There is, however, an extra Group which FISA now recognizes – Group S. Cars in this category can literally be anything at all, as the extra Group was introduced as an 'adjustment' by the authorities when it was realized there were not enough proper Group B, A or N cars in existence, let alone enough to fill a rally entry list.

On the organization side of these top-grade rallies, there are changes to the number and type of officials required. The hard core of Clerk of the Course, Secretary, Chief Marshal and Timekeeper continues, but is augmented by officials from the FISA. If the event qualifies for any FISA championship, a FISA-recognized and appointed Observer must attend and report back to Paris after the event has been run. Stewards are also required from overseas ASNs – and all the costs of bringing them to the event and, once there, keeping them in the 'manner to which they are accustomed', have to be borne by the rally organizers.

Regulations for Internationals are laid out in a different predetermined form than those of lesser-grade events and a standardized marking system is adopted which includes cash fines as well as time and exclusion penalties. They are often printed in more than one language, but the FISA only recognizes the French translation in the event of any difficulties arising. If a competitor has a grievance, this addition of an extra governing body gives him a further avenue of complaint, but it is a costly and complicated route to follow.

In Britain, we have an Open International Championship, which allows the relevant licence-holders from any other country in the world to compete in its rounds. Some of the qualifying rounds also form part of the FISA-recognized European Rally Championship, and consequently their rules are slightly more complex than the others. All cars competing in the Open series have to be homologated, and converting a 'club' rally car to its correct recognized specification can be an expensive operation. It does, however, provide the benefit of competing on an equal level with other cars, and of

An old factory Triumph TR7 V8 showing the high standard of preparation needed for international rallying.

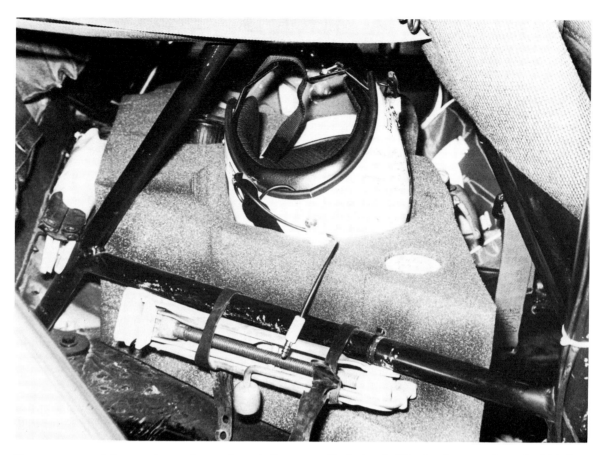

There never seems to be enough space in any rally car, but here, one of the factory Audi Quattros has a neat foam plastic bin fitted behind the front seats where helmets and spares are kept safely out of harm's way. (*Bishop*)

course the attraction of challenging the factory drivers in a similar car can lead to greater things for an ambitious driver.

The co-driver has even more of an office manager's job on his hands in the field of Internationals. Along with the increased status of a rally goes reams of extra paperwork, starting with the entry form and applying for licences and permits. In previous grades of rally, the co-driver has held a separate licence, but for Internationals there is but one – the International Rally Licence, gained by upgrading previous licences *i.e.* having them signed by organizers as proof of finishing rallies. The International Licence allows the co-driver to drive the car in competition, something not granted under lesser licences. Of course, they cost more than previous licences, as do corresponding Entrant's Licences and Advertising Permits. Entry forms are scrutinized more thoroughly at this level and entry fees have to be paid promptly – the closing dates for entry also have to be strictly adhered to, as in the past even factory drivers have been refused an entry on the grounds of it being received too late.

Route details are issued in advance of the rally start to allow competitors (usually co-drivers) to plan their rally thoroughly. But unless practising is allowed, extreme penalties are imposed if competitors are found on any of the special stages detailed in the road book before the event is run. A full schedule of the event is given by the road book, along with details of the route, usually in Tulip diagram form, supplemented by a list of map references of controls. From this information, a schedule of servicing arrangements can be drawn up and from a knowledge of which special stages are being used, some idea of tyre requirements can also be gained. The co-driver now takes on the mantle of team manager in pulling together the various elements of the team before the rally starts.

We are, perhaps, lucky in Britain to have such a good RAC National Championship on which to cut our teeth ready for Internationals. Thanks to this, it is not such a harrowing experience to take the step up to the higher grade of event. Everything is generally bigger than with a National; there may be extra hotels to book when the rally stops for a rest

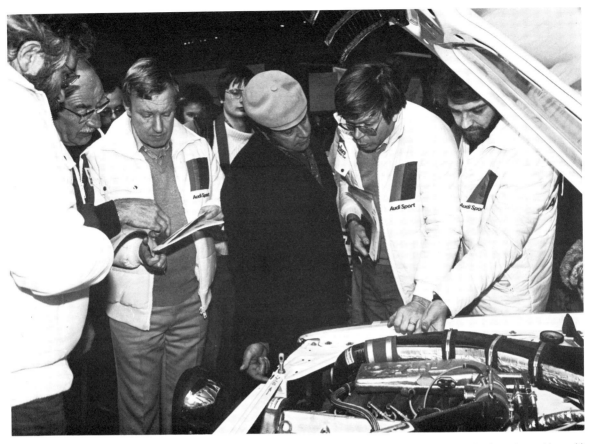

Even the factory teams can have problems at scrutineering. Officials on the 1982 Mintex International point out a problem with Hannu Mikkola's Quattro to co-driver Arne Hertz and German factory manager Roland Gumpert, whilst David Sutton tries to examine the homologation papers with scrutineer Jeff Ward. (*Large*)

halt away from its base, and your service crew will need precise instructions to follow in order to be in the right place at the right time in an area of the country they may have never visited before. Because Internationals can span many days and many hundreds of miles, the need for better planning is essential.

The actual on-event work is similar to that found on a top National Championship rally, but your first event may go something like this. You should arrive for scrutineering at your allowed time (there will be a penalty imposed if you don't) and although proceedings may seem to be a little lax, this is made up for at the event finish, when class-winning cars may be subjected to a thorough strip-down by an RAC-recognized Eligibility Scrutineer. Just the basic requirements for safety are usually checked at pre-event scrutiny, along with Advertising Permits – the officials are only looking for the obvious rule infraction before the rally. After the rally they are looking for detailed, and hidden, aspects of the car's specification.

Following scrutiny will be the normal documentation check, and an Identity Card will be issued for each car and crew. This will need passport-sized photographs of both crew members attaching to it and must be carried in the car for the duration of the event – it is usually fixed to the inside of a rear side window. Your rally car will also need to be signwritten with the names of both crew members, together with blood groups and nationalities (usually by means of a national flag). If you don't know your blood group type, it is easy for your doctor to check it for you, but be prepared to pay for the service.

After all this checking, a label will be issued by the Scrutineer and it must be attached to the car – if it is not intact at the finish, the car could be excluded. You will find that the engine has also been marked with special paint, just to make sure the block and cylinder head have not been changed during the course of the rally, as International rules dictate.

Scrutineering may take place the day before the rally starts and will give you a little extra time to sort yourself out. The rally car can be worked on after scrutineering and you will probably be having radios fitted to aid communications between rally car and service back-up crews. These will be checked at scrutineering by a Post Office official to ensure the correct frequency is being used and that a current licence is held. After the last car has been scrutineered, a list of starters will be issued by the organizers, together with individual starting times. This start list could differ from the original entry list. Certain conditions are laid down for the seeding of starters, with FISA-graded drivers ('A' or 'B' seeds) at the the front, followed by the various ASN-graded drivers, then the remainder. On World Championship rallies, such as the Lombard RAC, the FISA dictates that start lists should be compiled in Group order following the FISA-seeded drivers – first Group B, followed in order by Groups A and N.

The start list will be displayed at Rally HQ, together with the Official Noticeboard and examples of route definition arrows and control boards. It is now your responsiblity to arrive at the start on time, which could be at a later time than your car is due there. Most regulations state that cars should be placed in a closed park (*parc ferme*) for a certain amount of time before the start. Rules in a *parc ferme* are extremely strict in their enforcement. It should state in the regulations whether or not a member of the service crew can place the car in *parc ferme* before the start, or whether it has to be the crew itself. If it allows a mechanic to do it, take advantage of the extra time available to relax before the 'off'.

Route amendments can often be issued on Internationals. Bjorn Cederberg checks this Welsh Rally road book before the start in 1983. (*Large*)

Stage arrowing is the same on Internationals as on smaller British events. It looks like Stig Blomqvist is about to attack this arrow on the 1982 Scottish International. (*Bishop*)

Cars will generally start at one-minute intervals, but you may not be given your time cards until you present yourself and the car at the start control. However, an example of the time cards will already have been displayed at Rally HQ, so you should be familiar with their layout.

Once on the rally, the timing system in the Open series is standardized as target timing. Control procedure will be the same as on previous stage events, but here again, will be strictly policed. A control will be preceded by a yellow control board (picturing a clock face); this marks the border of the control area – pass that board and you are deemed to have entered the control and you will be penalized for early arrival. In Britain, the car is allowed to enter the control during the minute preceding your due arrival time, although the co-driver is allowed to enter the control on foot at any time. A marshal will only issue a time if the car and crew are in the vicinity of the control point (marked by a red board showing a clock face). If you cannot enter the control area on time – perhaps there has been a delay in starting the stage and the queue has built up down the road – you should present your time card to the marshal at the correct time and explain the situation, asking for a

delay allowance to be given, although nine times out of ten, the marshal will simply book you in and ask you to wait in the queue. That time spent queuing is then 'dead' time and cannot be penalized – after all, it's not your fault you can't start the stage on time. A control area is also considered to be a type of *parc ferme*, so no work is allowed to be carried out on the car except changing a damaged tyre and cleaning the windscreen and lamp glasses.

At a time control before a special stage start, you will be allotted a stage start time a minimum of three minutes later than your arrival time under FISA regulations. If you are unable to start the stage on time, penalties will be imposed, just as they will be if your car's engine is not running. The Special Stage Start is indicated by another red board, this time with a plain flag marked on it. Once clear of the stage start control, a yellow board with a plain flag and diagonal lines marked on it will indicate the control area limit.

Special stage marking will be the same as on lesser rallies, the only noticeable difference on Internationals being the presence of more marshals and spectators. At the end of the stage you will be timed across a flying finish line (that's the time to

Service areas are often packed with spectators and it can be quite difficult for a crew to locate its mechanics. In cases like these, it is a good idea to send a mechanic to the arrival control where he can tell the rally crew exactly where the barge can be found. Distinctive boards placed on the roofs of service barges also help rally crews to find their mechanics. (*Bishop*)

stop your stopwatch). The approach of a flying finish is marked by a yellow board depicting a chequered flag, usually placed about 100 metres before the line itself. The position of the flying finish line is marked with an identical board, but this time in red. There may then be a countdown of 3-2-1 to the actual finish control (marked by a red 'Stop' board) where you should stop to receive your time. The time you receive will also be the start time for the following road section, to which you add the target time to find your due arrival time at the next control. You should, of course, check the marshal's clock. You are clear of the finish control as soon as you pass the yellow board marked with diagonal lines.

Passage controls are frequently used on Internationals and serve the purpose of doubling as a card collection point. They can be positioned after every special stage to allow stage time cards to be collected and fed to the results team back at Rally HQ. These controls are marked in the same way with yellow and red boards, but this time depicting a rubber stamp.

The next oddity with Internationals comes at a

rest halt – rules dictate that crews must have a break after 300 miles of rallying. Where previously the only halt has been the likes of half an hour at a lunchtime service halt, you could now have a stop-over of several hours. Controls will be placed before and after the halt and cars will enter a *parc ferme* for the interval. Generally speaking, there is a lengthy service period before and sometimes after the halt. During these halts one of two things will take place: either Regrouping or Reclassification. Regrouping is a simple closing-up of gaps in the field to restart cars at one-minute intervals in the exact order they entered the regrouping control. Reclassification, on the other hand, concerns the restarting of cars in their correct overall position order.

FISA states that a field cannot be reclassified before one-third of the special stage mileage has been covered, so with compact Open Championship rounds, this rarely takes place. Instead, cars are regrouped, but it can have a severe effect on cars running down the field. If there have been many retirements early in a rally, crews running at the tail end could find they are due out of a regroup control

Arne Hertz and Fred Gallagher check their stage times on the 1983 Lombard RAC Rally, with Phil Short and Ian Grindrod doing the same in the background. (*Bishop*)

only minutes after arriving. For example, say you started the rally as the 100th car and 45 cars have retired in front of you. If the regroup is over a 60-minute rest period, you will only have 16 minutes! This is because cars are still restarted at one-minute intervals, and instead of being the 100th car, as you were at the rally start, you are now the 56th, so you will restart 56 minutes behind the first car, not 100 minutes – the difference is now 44 minutes, and that difference is subtracted from the rest halt period to give your new restart time; hence the 16 minutes rest! It's tough at the bottom, isn't it?

Now even though a rally may be past its one-third stage distance, there could still be insufficient time to reclassify the field in order to run a compact event. The time needed to reclassify depends on how late the very last car of the rally is running on the road, for until its penalties are known, the result cannot be calculated and hence a reclassified field cannot restart. For this reason, reclassification usually only takes place after an overnight rest halt. In either case, the officials will inform each crew of its new restart time – with regrouping, the time is given as you enter the *parc ferme*, whilst with reclassifying

your new start time is posted on an Official Noticeboard and it is up to you to find out that time. Whilst the car is in a *parc ferme*, the crew must leave it immediately and must not return until a few minutes before the restart time. No work is permitted on the car in the *parc ferme* unless specified by the organizers on safety grounds, when it is carried out in the presence of an official – time taken for such work is penalized as if it was a road penalty.

If there is a lengthy service period immediately before an overnight halt, some organizers will allow a member of the service crew to place the car in the *parc ferme* which follows, permitting you and your driver to grab a few extra minutes' rest. This is one ruling you should definitely take note of and use to your advantage – rest is a valuable commodity on long rallies.

Maximum Permitted Lateness also differs on larger events. There could be an overall cumulative lateness allowance covering the entire event, but there would also be an allowance given between each major control (rest halt). They could, of course, be the same allowance, but it should be remembered that for each section of the rally after a restart, a competitor's road lateness returns to zero. For example, take a rally with four section (or legs) where the maximum permitted lateness is 30 minutes on any section, but there is no cumulative maximum lateness. That means a crew can be up to 30 minutes late at the end of each leg without being excluded, even though their cumulative lateness at the finish could be 120 minutes. Some events allow a penalty-free lateness period, whilst others penalize any lateness – usually at the rate of a 10-seconds time penalty for each minute late.

Lateness only applies, of course, to road sections, but if a competitor exceeds the target time for a special stage, he can expect to have that particular excess over target time counted as road penalties. The crew will then be credited with a special stage penalty equal to that particular stage's target time. Under the target timing system, lateness is always cumulative within a section and cannot be reduced by booking in early – once lost, time cannot be regained.

That, in a nutshell, is International rallying in Britain. Events naturally have more atmosphere than any of the National rallies, but there are basically few differences – as said before – so good is the National rally scene. There will, however, be more trade awareness on the larger events, and you should keep your eyes open for any deals that are likely to be offered for using individual products. Tyre, component and oil companies often offer bonus schemes where individual rally results (say class positions) could win some cash or a few free tyres, all in exchange for a signature on a contract or for merely displaying the right stickers on your car. As you progress in the sport and the results improve, you should learn just how valuable advertising space on your car can be worth to a sponsor. In Britain, the RAC Open Championship enjoyed good guaranteed television coverage at the time of writing, although the national dailies in Fleet Street still needed a little more encouragement to allow rallying space on their sports pages. You should, of course, do your utmost to give any sponsors a return for their interest by keeping local press, radio and television abreast of your activities. If your backer has invested more than a couple of thousands of pounds in your effort, you could even consider asking a PR agency to issue press releases on your behalf. It may sound all pie in the sky to the average clubman, but it is a competitive sport and if you are the least bit ambitious you should look back to the opening sentence of this chapter . . . read it once again, and now start to act as they do!

11

Internationals Abroad

Once you possess an International-status Competition Licence, the entire world is literally open to you, but it is an idea to cut your teeth on a home International first. Timing systems are fairly standard throughout the world, and as event regulations are generally printed in English as a secondary language, any differences should be apparent. If, however, a foreign organizer does not produce an English version of the ASRs, then give the event a miss – you could be opening a can of worms by entering.

Your primary requirement to compete on a foreign rally is permission from the RAC MSA. This will be granted by way of a visa for any rally listed in the FISA International Rally Calendar. Of course, a fee is payable and at the time of writing it was about £11. Separate visas will be needed for driver and co-driver, and your rally entry form will also need to be stamped by the RAC. Rally organizers usually ask for a couple of passport-sized photographs of the driver and co-driver to be forwarded as well, together with homologation details of the car you intend to use. If you are co-driving for a foreign driver abroad, all you require is a visa – there is no need to have an entry list sent to you for RAC stamping.

When taking your entire equipe abroad, you can expect to be thoroughly checked at the customs posts of any countries visited. Because your service barge is packed with spares and tyres, the customs men will treat them as imports, and consequently will need some kind of bond as an assurance that you are not about to sell any of them to the locals – ironically, spares are generally cheaper on the Continent anyway! You could, of course, pay the bond, which can run to several thousands of pounds if the rally car is taken into consideration as well, but your money will be tied up for quite a time and could

take months to recover. By far the best way of overcoming the problem is to take a carnet, which lists in infinite detail everything carried in the service barge. Carnets are available from your local Chamber of Commerce. But if you think you are escaping the bureaucratic red tape easily, think again. These carnets have to be stamped both on entry to and exit from a country – if a stamp is missing, the next customs post along your route will turn you round and send you back to collect it. The big problem is that some customs posts close on Sundays and most can be interminably laborious in carrying out their duties at the best of times. The golden rule is never to plan for a rapid dash across Europe, but to allow an extra half day for delays.

Another useful check before you leave home is for continental public holidays. Our European friends enjoy many more days off than we do in Britain, and this has to be taken into consideration when planning for a week-long practice session before the event – trying to find petrol for a practice car on a foreign bank holiday can prove to be a fruitless quest.

Because rules have been standardized by the FISA the only major differences between an International in Britain and one abroad are the scenery and the language, but some countries do have peculiarities.

Scandinavia
The Scandinavian countries, Finland in particular, produce some of the world's best rally drivers and consequently the sport is extremely popular and enthusiastically followed. The enthusiasm is shared by rally officials, who invariably enforce every rule to the letter. In both Finland and Sweden the majority of rallies are 'secret', just as in Britain. They enjoy rallying on snow and ice-covered roads in the winter

Competing abroad can open up whole new opportunities for gaining more experience. Dean Senior, one of the British Junior Team drivers, tackles the Swedish International in 1984 and learns how to use studded tyres on snow and ice. (*Bishop*)

Just across the channel there are many opportunities to try pacenoted tarmac rallying at very low cost. The excitement of fast tarmac rallying is captured here by Michele Lizin, driving a borrowed factory Citroen Visa in Belgium. (*Bishop*)

and dry dusty gravel tracks during the summer – and each produces its own special problems.

On a winter rally in Scandinavia, approach roads to special stages can be narrow and lined with high snow banks where ploughs have opened the road. It always pays to arrive at stages with plenty of time in hand, otherwise you could find yourself at the wrong end of a lengthy queue. The marshals generally understand the problem and book you in at the correct time, but some are so enthusiastic, they will wait for your car to enter the control area before clocking you in. Servicing on these rallies, as with most foreign events, is much freer than in Britain. You may only have an official service area at the end of a leg before a rest halt; for the rest of the event you have to arrange your own roadside service and take the time from your road section target time. Most rallies use target timing from one special stage start to another, instead of from the finish of one to the start of another – this effectively turns the event into a road race as well. Scandinavian countries do, however, strictly enforce the normal speed limit on public roads, and police with radar traps are a common sight – if you exceed the limit, expect an on-the-spot fine and a further delay by answering 'just a few routine questions, Sir'.

Strict control procedure needs to be followed. You are allowed to enter a control area during the

Cars have to be prepared specially for each type of rally. This is a factory Nissan in Safari Rally trim, with a boot packed with tow rope, winch, steel cable . . . and a pair of wellington boots! (*Bishop*)

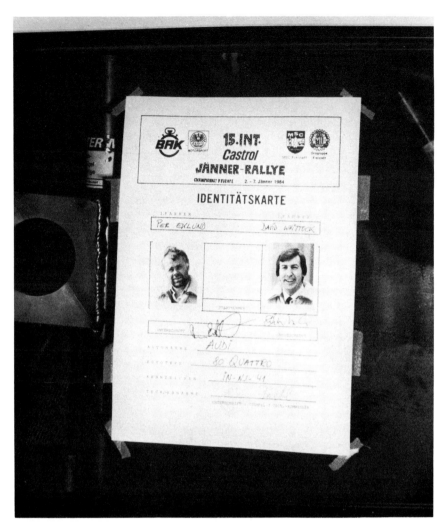

minute before your due time, but you are booked in the instant you hand over the time card for signing. One second too early and you are given the previous minute – there is none of this handing over the card and asking the marshal for the next minute as sometimes happens in Britain. Treat the marshals as machines, not human beings.

The Rally HQ will generally be a local hotel, and the Official Noticeboard will be displayed there. You can expect a very high standard of organization and there is rarely a bad event within the Scandinavian calendar – it is, however, an expensive place to get to from Britain, and once there, both food and hotels are on the pricey side, too. But for undulating roads not seen in any other country, a visit to Scandinavia should be included in every rallyman's programme at some time or other.

Mainland Europe

Your first foreign rally will probably be in either Belgium, Germany, France or Holland. These countries are easy to reach from Britain and organizers of rallies there are usually delighted to see you – so much so that they will generally give you free entries and pay for your hotels – some even pay start money to attract you in the first place. It seems they like the sideways driving style of British drivers, and after watching some of the locals, you will soon understand why!

Belgium or Holland are the best to start with. Their rallies are usually all tarmac and all practice. When making pacenotes, particular attention should be given to road sections as well as stages. These rallies usually run on a lapping system of several special stages, the rally returning to a town square central control after each lap – and it is there that the problem occurs. Spectators tend to charge around following the rally, and if the rally is in town, their sole aim is to be there as well. The top runners can normally manage to slip through before the hordes arrive, but lower numbers can get caught up in massive traffic jams – it is then time to take to the footpath or any other hard ground which isn't occupied at that time! It is usually a good idea to familiarize yourself fully with the side roads of the town where the rally is based – they can provide a useful escape route.

Service schedules are not easily planned on these events, although it is normally safe to allow road sections to be covered at an average speed of 60km/h. Service crews have to learn to work extremely quickly, and thought should be given to packing the barge in a certain way. In a British event there will invariably be plenty of time to load and unload the barge at service areas, but on foreign rallies everything hinges around speed, so it is no help if a trolley jack and axle stands are hidden away under a pile of tyres and fuel cans at the bottom of the van.

Special stages on these events have often been branded as uninteresting – just a series of straights and 90-degree bends over flat country. However, this opinion does them an injustice; they can contain a great variety of stages and should not be underestimated. It is true that an event has to be chosen carefully; some Belgian rallies, in particular,

have a reputation for including ridiculously rough roads. However, on the whole, stages will be over good-quality tarmac, but also featuring a number of concrete roads and sections over cobbles (*pavé*). The gravel content of stages generally refers to mud roads – fine in dry weather, when racing tyres can still be used, but if it rains, the only answer is to use forest tyres! Concrete roads tend to be slippery when dry as they are covered with a light coating of dust, whilst *pavé* is slippery all the time. When making pacenotes, all these changes in road surface need to be recorded prominently. There are few kerbstones lining tarmac roads, but concrete roads often have a shear, sharp-edged step down at their sides just waiting to tear out the wall of a racing tyre. Roads across open countryside tend to flood very quickly in rain; as few of the fields have proper drainage, all of this water is channelled down the roads – the water also washes slimey mud on to the roads. There are rarely any stage arrows to be found – spectators regard them as souvenirs and pinch them before the rally even arrives!

Controls are again strictly marshalled, but crews can usually hand over their time cards before due time without the marshal 'doing' them for booking in

Basic checks on cars, like this noise check on the Hunsruck Rally in Germany, still have to be carried out at International level. Some of the exhaust pipes have been blocked off on this Porsche 911SC. (*Bishop*)

Control procedure can be stricter on foreign rallies. Here, cars queue at a stage arrival control in Germany. The driver of the VW Golf is really bending the rules by stopping after the yellow 25m control board. Drivers usually wait by their cars as co-drivers walk to the control table to wait for their correct time, calling their drivers forward when it is time to book in. (*Large*)

early. The marshals do, however, watch carefully for cars crossing into the control area too early. Rally HQ is rarely at a hotel, as there are not too many in existence; instead, the organization is usually based in one of the host town's public buildings, with an Official Noticeboard in a cafe where crews usually gather for a chat with other competitors – in Holland and Belgium, rallying has a very casual and amenable atmosphere attached to it.

In France, rallying is much more matter-of-fact. The stages of tarmac rallies are usually of a very high standard, particularly in the Alps, where small Internationals frequently run over Monte Carlo Rally stages. Rally HQ before the event is usually based at the promoting club's offices (in France almost every Automobile Club has a permanent office), but during the rally it generally moves to a hotel or public building.

Servicing on French events is free, and on some of the larger rallies, where stages can run up to 60km in length, top teams organize pit stops mid-stage to change tyres. Timing is more refined than in Holland and Belgium, still using the target system, but with better road section allowances. Printing clocks are widely used at stage arrival controls, where a co-driver has to stamp his own time card at the correct time. As in Holland and Belgium, stages are not arrowed at all. There is rarely any penalty-free lateness allowed on these rallies – and foreign competitors do not need to use those ridiculous yellow driving lamps.

Italy is about the same as France, but gravel roads are featured more often. However, spectator problems can be immense. Hordes of them line the stages and on road sections it often seems that all of Italy is following the rally – passionately! It is best to adopt a 'when in Rome . . .' approach and use your horn a lot. Timing is again target between stage start and stage start, but delays on these link sections are so unpredictable that it is a case of 'grande attack' everywhere – fortunately, the police are all rally fanatics, too!

Portugal and Spain produce a mixture of tarmac and gravel-based rallies, and again are plagued with suicidal spectators with an inherent interest in causing traffic jams at the drop of a hat. These

A co-driver waits for the right time to appear before clocking her own time card with this printing clock. This type of clock is very popular in Germany and France. (*Large*)

A *parc ferme* at a regrouping control on the Antibes Rally in the South of France. Cars are kept safe for several hours, with crews barred from returning to them until a few minutes before they are due to depart – no work is allowed to be carried out on the cars in a *parc ferme*. (*Bishop*)

blockages may not hamper the rally (it is almost a Cardinal Sin to delay a rally car), but your service crew will undoubtedly have its work cut out in keeping to a tight schedule. On all Mediterranean rallies, thought should be given to using one service barge for major services and a fast small estate car for emergency service. Road sections can often cross several steep mountain passes over roads with which a car could cope easily, but which would bring a

service barge's average speed down to about 25km/h.

Of the other European countries, Germany probably has the biggest rally following, but it still attracts nowhere near the number that events in France, Italy and Belgium do: which is ironic, really, when you consider how motor car-orientated is German industry. Good events are few and far between, usually having to be restricted to military

Spectators can be a problem abroad, where rallying is much more popular than in Britain. It is difficult to spot the rally car in the crowded scene (above) from the Boules de Spa Rally in Belgium. (*Bishop*) Some rallies even include passage controls like this example (below) in the middle of special stages. The co-driver is holding out his time card for the marshal to stamp. (*Bishop*)

land for special stages, which can mean extremely rough gravel tracks and very fast tarmac roads. Although Germany has gigantic forests, conservation groups have the ear of the Government and are largely instrumental in having them barred from rally use. Timing is normally by printing clock at arrival controls, but control procedures can be a little lax. However, stages tend to be arrowed. Practising can be severely restricted on German events run over military land, but it is quite common for the first day of a rally to use the following day's stages as road sections, which thereby allows a crew to make rough pacenotes.

Eastern Bloc countries are always enthusiastically seeking crews from the West to enter their rallies, but the standard of competition can be poor in comparison with other European events. Stages usually feature a round-the-houses town centre test, where the entire population will turn out to spectate. Tarmac, *pavé* and gravel stages can be found in each rally, and because of the organizers' enthusiasm, you will be sure of a warm, friendly welcome – and probably a financially rewarding one, too.

Further afield

Rallying in the Middle East sounds expensive, but an event could be tackled for about the same cost as the Scottish or the Circuit of Ireland. The Middle East Championship is now recognized by the FISA, so regulations have been standardized, and organizers normally welcome foreign entrants. Special stages can vary from tarmac roads to indefinable desert tracks and provide crews with a real rallying adventure. Cars must be prepared well to withstand some pretty rough going. Tackling a Middle East rally is almost like stepping back in time in British rallying in terms of the social atmosphere and camaraderie amongst competitors – and the Arab peoples' generous hospitality has to be witnessed to be believed. Because of the nature of some desert roads, passage controls are quite a common inclusion along a stage route.

The United States of America, too, provides a competitive rallying field with its SCCA Pro Rally series. Events are run along the lines of European rallies, but special stages tend to be long (15 to 20-mile stages are the norm) and are grouped together with no allowance for servicing. Consequently, cars have to be reliable and tyres hard-wearing – European-type tyres wear too quickly to be competitive. There are usually strict controls on servicing, and most events use totally gravel-based stages. Within the rallying world, the USA has been branded with an 'amateur' status in the past, but things have changed and rallying is rapidly becoming a very professional and popular sport over there. In terms of a European-based crew travelling to events across the Atlantic, careful planning could see hundreds of pounds saved in freight charges.

Almost every country in the world promotes rallying, and with organization and regulations all of the same standard, there is no reason why, after a little careful planning, a crew with a taste for adventure should not compete on several continents in a single year. With that sort of experience under your belt, you would be fodder for motor club after-dinner talks for months – and you would undoubtedly gain more backing from sponsors.

12

Team Management

It may sound very grand for a clubman team to have a manager, but it is a worthwhile addition. Although not in the class of John Davenport, Peter Ashcroft, Dave Richards, Tony Fall or David Sutton, every team should have a central figure who assumes overall control during an event – usually an experienced co-driver or driver who still wants to be involved with the sport, but not too actively. An efficient team manager can take the load off any co-driver's shoulders, but it doesn't mean the co-driver has no say in decision-making. He is still involved in pre-event planning activities, such as service and tyre schedules, booking accommodation and submitting entry forms, but he is relieved of some on-event work, which in theory should allow him more time to concentrate on pure co-driving.

A team manager can be in places a co-driver cannot. He can sit at the end of stages to check other competitors' times, or hang around service areas after his car has left to make sure rivals don't bend any rules. He is also a co-ordinator when the team has several cars, able to decide which service barge goes where in cases of drama, or deciding which car to throw every effort behind as the rally finish draws nearer.

A typical clubman team of two cars for something like the Lombard RAC Rally would have a support fleet similar to this: One service barge and one fast pursuit service car or chase car (probably a converted estate car), a tyre truck and a management car.

Service barge. Each service barge would have either two or three mechanics (one of them able to act as a proficient navigator) and should be in touch with the rest of the team by radio – if funds stretch that far. In the back of the van should be everything necessary to effectively rebuild the car and keep it in the rally

after the driver has enjoyed himself too much. Heavy items like compressors, welding equipment and fuel/water cans should be kept as close to the floor as possible to help lower the centre of gravity of the van – anyone following a fully laden service barge should do so warily, for although they look totally unwieldy, most can out-handle a normal road car and will probably out-accelerate it as well.

Racks of spare parts line the inside walls of barges, along with boxes of tools, jacks, axle stands and – most important – a kettle. Some even have a proper workbench and vices. On top of the van there is usually a strong rack for storing wheels and tyres, and maybe a few more cans of fuel, but the least carried on top the better for roadholding. Most vans also carry a generator to supply power to floodlights needed when servicing in darkness, although there are now several replacement alternators on the market which can out-produce small petrol-run generators.

The cab of a service barge should not be forgotten, either. Mechanics have to follow route instructions, too, so if funds permit, some thought should be given to fitting a tripmeter, while essential items include a map light, a strong interior light and decent seat belts and seats – a good set of auxiliary driving lamps is also useful and can be used as spares for the rally car. Thought should be given to a service board as well. These are used to identify the barge in a crowded service area and should, of course, be illuminated at night. The top teams can spend more time on preparing a service barge than on the rally car – both, incidentally, have to be reliable; it's no good having a rally car capable of lasting the distance if your service barge burns its clutch out trying to climb Sutton Bank!

Chase car. Although some organizers outlaw the

A well-laid-out service/chase car, with a full complement of tools and spares. (*Bishop*)

work carried out by chase cars, they cannot really ban them from events. All of the top teams use them and on some events abroad they are a vital part of any team. In Britain, servicing is generally confined to official areas, so the presence of a chase car in the middle of a large forest complex, such as Dalby or Kielder, does suggest skullduggery afoot. They will usually be the same model of car as the rally car, or a similar model using mostly suspension and transmission parts compatible with the rally car. Two mechanics would crew the chase car, the remaining space being taken up with spare wheels, fuel cans and vital spare parts which can be changed quickly (within say 10 to 15 minutes) to keep the car running until it can reach the proper service barge. If the work is carried out along the route, crews can expect to be excluded, but if the work is carried out just off the route, 'what the eye doesn't see . . .'

Between some extremely long special stages it is not uncommon for a rally car to come across a couple of wheels and a fuel can just dumped at the roadside. A crew with initiative would, of course, take advantage of this fortuitous windfall, leaving a pair of worn-out tyres and an empty fuel can behind, to be spirited away by a chase car. It has also been known

for mechanics to be taking a walk through the forest at that precise moment as well, but organizers' Judges of Fact are now appointed to patrol likely areas for this illegal servicing. When an official is patrolling, a marvellous game of 'cops and robbers' usually ensues, with competing cars trying to shake off their 'tails' and officials trying to flush-out mechanics from the undergrowth – with chase cars unable to return and pick them up until the official has disappeared!

There are legal uses of chase cars, though, for as long as they are not seen servicing a car, nobody can stop them shadowing a rally car on road sections, just in case . . . When the choice is between retirement or an illegal repair which, if found out, would mean exclusion, most teams would choose the latter. Chase cars can be used at official areas which proper barges cannot reach. Since you will not have the awesome number of barges a factory team has at its disposal, your barge and chase car will probably leap-frog along the route to provide adequate cover.

Tyre truck. Even a small team should consider the advantage of using a tyre truck. The economics of the sport at International level usually dictate that a

Continental rallies like the Boucles de Spa, in Belgium, are ideal for using both service barges and chase cars. Here, Robert Droogmans' Porsche 911SC RS sits behind its service barge, with the high-speed chase car, complete with tyres on the roof, alongside. (*Bishop*)

team will have a considerable number of part-worn tyres to transport around. If you are fortunate enough to have an arrangement with a tyre manufacturer to purchase tyres at a competitor's discount, you will probably be able to recover most of the cost of the new tyres by selling the part-worn covers to other competitors after the rally – as long as you have somewhere to keep them. The tyre truck need be nothing more than a hack rented van, which will only need to rendezvous with service barges at a few points around the route to collect old tyres and dispense new ones. Without this truck, your service barge will become weighed down with redundant wheels and tyres and its crew will have to waste time visiting the major manufacturers' tyre trucks, waiting for new covers to be fitted to wheels, when really they should be charging off down the route to the next service point. Although you only require a driver for the truck, it is best to give him a passenger for safety reasons, to share the driving and navigating.

Management car. Like the flagship of the fleet, the management car acts as the communications base for the team. The team manager will probably cover as much of the route as possible, arriving at strategic points early to organize everything. The car will carry the bare essentials of spares, but where paperwork is concerned it will be a mobile office. Full sets of documents relating to the event and vehicles will be carried and a set of up-to-date stage times for the team cars and their rivals will also be found there; everything to enable a vital change in plans to be made.

The management car should arrive at rest halts early enough for room reservations to be checked and for food for the crews to be arranged. Time can be saved if room keys are signed for in advance, then handed to the crews as they arrive at the 'In' control. The management car can be used as an extra set of eyes to watch the opposition. Occupants of a rival chase car being shadowed by your team manager would think twice before illegally servicing a rally car. It could also be used to gain information about route and stage conditions ahead, radioing details back to the rally car to aid tyre choice. If an important repair has taken longer than expected, the manager can drive on ahead of the rally car to check for traffic jams and short cuts. The list of uses is never-ending.

As teams become more professional in their approach to Internationals, the team expands. A few years ago, only the factory teams could afford motorhomes, but ever more privateers are finding them invaluable. Apart from the obvious prestige value of a caravanette or motorhome, it enables food to be readily available for competitors and service crew alike and there is always somewhere quiet to sit down and relax for a while, or somewhere for mechanics to thaw out after the inevitable wet and windy service area in Kielder. A motorhome could even save money if it is large enough to be used as a mobile hotel – rest halts and Rally HQs invariably centre around a four-star hotel with accompanying high-cost rooms.

So much for the sort of vehicles you could include in your team; next comes the mountain of paperwork which needs to be prepared before the rally. Apart from the rally entry form and homologation papers for your car, you will need to compile various schedules for each faction within the team. Planning these schedules can begin weeks before the rally starts, but most depend to a large extent on the detailed rally timetable. Movement schedules detailing who is where and when can be written as soon as you have a rough outline of the rally, but service schedules and tyre schedules cannot be drawn up until the road book is issued. Loading forms for service barges and chase cars may also need altering from event to event, then there are hotel reservations to be made and possibly ferries to be booked, or air tickets arranged.

Entry forms and homologation papers

Entry forms for major rallies should be considered carefully; the information contained on them is likely to be your only link with the organizers. If you have sufficient results from previous events, detail them (on a separate sheet if you like) to enable the organizers to seed you in the appropriate starting position. All elements of the form should be completed and a check should be made to see if entries are accepted on a 'first come, first served' basis, otherwise you may have to wait until a selection committee has decided who should and who shouldn't be allowed to compete – in the latter case, any forms not correctly filled in will be the first to be discarded.

Careful consideration of which class to enter should also be made. Some International-status rallies do not have to run to FISA Championship regulations and so can allow the older Groups 2 and 4 cars to run in their own classes. Some of the more popular cars can quickly be converted from their Group A or B trim to the original Group 2 or 4 specification with little modification (in some cases no mods at all). If you think there is likely to be less competition in one of the older classes and the prize-money is the same, it could be worthwhile entering that class, but it is doubtful whether you would be able to gain any points towards championships when using these 'older' cars.

In all cases, you should pay the required entry fee in full – failure to do this is a serious offence which would lose you your Competition Licence. Various Entrant's and Advertising Licences and permits are obtainable from the RAC MSA, and if competing

Team managers keep up-to-date records of stage times for all cars and constantly stay in touch with their team. From the left, Terry Harryman, Jochen Berger, Fred Gallagher, Gunter Wanger and Henri Toivonen. (*Bishop*)

It is the co-driver's job to explain route details to the service crews by running through a service schedule and pointing out locations of service areas on a map. (*Bishop*)

abroad you will need the RAC's permission by way of a visa.

Rallies usually offer prospective entrants a lower entry fee for returning forms early, say two months before the event is run. Then entries at the 'normal' rate are usually accepted up to about one month before the start – these dates have to be strictly adhered to and it is not uncommon for factory teams to send someone along with their entry to place it personally in the organizer's hands. There are usually two separate forms – one for private entrants and one for trade entrants. Again the difference between these should be considered, and maybe a new Entrant's Licence needs to be obtained. Your sponsorship agreement could include a Trade Entrant's Licence for the year, but it could be that this particular rally is offering attractive prize-money for private entrants; a quick chat with your backers to explain the situation could result in an increased bag of gold at the finish.

The entry form will ask for details of the competing car, along with its homologation number. Details of cars eligible for international rallying are obtainable from the FISA in Paris, or from the RAC

MSA, and copies of the relevant homologation papers can be purchased from the car manufacturer concerned, usually from its Competitions Department. These homologation papers should be kept with the rally car for the duration of the rally and may be checked by an official at any time. You should, of course, check with the manufacturer in plenty of time before the intended rally that he has made no further modifications or changes to the official specification – if he has, then you will need to obtain the extra homologation sheets to supplement your original papers.

You should take photocopies of all entry forms submitted and, whether the organizers have asked for it or not, include a brief résumé of your competition career (couched in a lighthearted manner). Internationals will invariably have commentators speaking to the public at scrutineering and on spectator special stages, and any information you can give them will ease their work load and consequently will be accepted gratefully. Rally organizers also send out regular Press Releases concerning entries received to date. If you think you can't handle it yourself, try

On most continental rallies, it is a case of service wherever you can. Roadside services like this can quite often include major jobs like an axle change. (*Bishop*)

approaching one of the smaller PR companies which specialize in that sort of thing – they could probably come up with a novel idea to promote you in the public eye, and at a surprisingly reasonable cost as well.

Movement schedule
Regulations will include a detailed timetable of the rally and should include a rough route outline. If not, contact the organizers and ask for one – the factory teams will!

From this information, you can draw up a rough schedule for planning the movement of various team personnel and vehicles, maybe weeks before the rally takes place. These schedules are invaluable for foreign rallies, or when you may conscript part-time team members for a particular rally. It sets out in black and white who is where and when. The schedule, of course, will depend on the outcome of travel bookings such as ferries, flights and hotel reservations, and it can take quite a time to compile.

Each team member should be given an individual sheet detailing their particular movements, together with a complete list of movements for the entire team. The list will detail which hotels are being used, booking-in times for ferries or flights, together with relevant telephone numbers to use if anything either goes wrong or becomes delayed. In fact, any information to help any team individual in difficulty should be included on a movement schedule.

Service schedule
A service schedule cannot be drawn up until precise route details are known, as it details exactly where each service barge or chase car has to be and when it has to be there, and gives an idea of what sort of work is to be carried out. In British Internationals, the route will be detailed in a road book, and these are generally only available a week or so before the event – on pacenote rallies, however, this can be extended to about a month before the start.

When road books are issued, the factory teams will normally send someone to collect them, saving the precious day or two that the postal service would normally take to deliver them. Work starts immediately in transferring the route to a small-scale map of the entire rally area. In such a way, some idea as to the overall complexity of the route can be gained. The rally Regs will state whether or not servicing is restricted to official service areas governed by 'In' and 'Out' controls, in which case there may be a time restriction imposed. If servicing is not restricted in such a way, it could be allowed off the public highway in places like garages or workshops, but prior permission *must* be obtained from their owners. Factory teams usually have lists of contacts at garages and workshops around the country, which allows them to book their space as soon as details of the route are known. Other events have no restrictions on servicing at all.

When planning a schedule, the official service areas should be considered first, then garages or workshops, but in either case your servicing should take place as close to the following time control as possible. There is always some discussion concerning whether or not to service immediately after or immediately before a stage. This is where a chase car reveals its usefulness. If a car strikes trouble, in most cases it will be on a special stage. Now, if service arrangements have been made at the end of the following road section, the rally car may be so badly damaged it would never reach service. On the other hand, if servicing is arranged immediately after a stage, any damage can be put right straight away, but the rally car could be delayed by traffic jams on the following road section. It is therefore best to arrange some sort of emergency servicing close to a stage finish, leaving the main servicing to a point closer to the following control.

Road timing should be slack enough to take service requirements into consideration, but a team should be prepared for perhaps only five or 10 minutes for unofficial service, as opposed to the half-hour or so at an official service halt. The

Audi Sport UK		Supv. One DS/GR Supv. Two Service One RL/WM/JB Service Two JO'C/AM Service Three SS/PR		Q AV LT LT	Service Four Service Five Service Six Tyre Truck Pirelli Fiat Motorhome LS/PB Bedouin			**David Sutton Motorsport Ltd.** SERVICE SCHEDULE 2nd LEG - 1 EVENT SCOTTISH							
Crew No.	SV. PT.	Road Book/ Map Ref.	Location	Aft SS	At TC	Arrv By	1st car due	Routing	R/car Dist. to next	Ser Time	Dir App	p	Tyres	Special Comments
Ser 1 (Ser 2)	55 E	64/ 581653 89-0.00	Holiday Inn, Glasgow Re-start	-	TC 28 B	08.40	MON 09.00	-	-	-	-	-	-	Ser 1 release Ser 2 as soon as rally car starts OK. Ser 1 follow to next.
Sup Ser 3 Ser 1 (Ser 2)	56	73/ 238406 before 95-55.37	Lay by on A72, just before Peebles	bef 29	-	09.45	10.20	M74, A72 Lanark, A743 A70, A721 A72 (55)	R: 26 S: 24 3 grav	15 min	W	65 lit	(NT) 2 spares	Ser 2 pass thro' non-stop if OK. Ser 1 follow to next.
Ser 1	57 E	73/ 312369 97-0.09	Exit Stage 29 B 7062	29	-	asap	10.55	B7062	-	-	NW	-	-	Care - narrow roads. Beware marshals PC29. Follow to next.
Ser 1	58 E	73/ 404361 99-0.05	Exit Stage 30 yellow road	30	-	asap	11.25	B7062, B709 yellow road	-	-	SE	-	-	Care - narrow roads. Follow to next.
Ser 1	59 E	73/ 469323 101-0.06	Exit Stage 31 A707	31	-	asap	11.50	yellow road A707	-	-	SE	-	-	Care - narrow roads. Follow to service
Sup Ser 2,3 Ser 1 MH	60	73/ 477274 after 102-4.52	Lay by on A7 after passage control	31	PC 31	11.00	11.55	As S.Pt.56, then A72, A707, Selkirk (80) W roads only	R: 24 S: 9 1 grav	20 min	NW	50 lit	NT 1 spare	Ser 3 leave as soon as rally car arrives OK. Ser 1 do not follow rally car.
Ser 1	61 E	79/ 279099 105-0.78	Exit Stage 32	32	-	asap	12.55	B 7009 B 709	-	-	E	-	-	Follow to service

This example of a service schedule was prepared for the Audi Sport UK team for the 1984 Scottish Rally. The columns are self-explanatory and, as can be seen, very comprehensive. In the service point column (SV. PT.), an 'E' depicts emergency service only as it is not an official service area. The R/car Dist. to next column indicates the road mileage (R) and stage mileage (S) to the next service point, together with the number of stages and whether these are tarmac or gravel. The columns following show roughly how much petrol will be required for the rally car and the type and number of tyres to be fitted. A well thought out service plan like this can make the difference between winning and losing a rally – on this occasion, Hannu Mikkola was driving the Audi Quattro rally car and he won!

logistics of moving service barges and chase cars around the route is the next thing to consider – it's no good having a superb schedule planned with service barges at the end of each stage if they are expected to average 50mph between rendezvous points!

On main roads, a service barge in good condition should be capable of averaging just over 30mph, but in narrow country lanes or hilly countryside, the speed would drop considerably. It should also be borne in mind that the mechanics will need to stop to refill fuel cans, eat, and possibly have new tyres fitted to wheels. They will also need time to unpack and repack the barge at every service point. If you are unfortunate enough to be using a barge with a tachograph fitted, the laws of the land will apply to the total number of hours it may be on the road and how long each driver is allowed to drive without a break.

Your service barges will have to display official rally plates to gain access to certain service areas, and you can expect to have to pay for extra plates. You can also be penalized for your service crew's misbehaviour on the road, for such things as speeding, or for leaving an official service route where one is detailed.

A good service schedule should be comprehensive and have precise details of where to position vehicles. Each service point should be given a reference number or letter, along with a note of which vehicle is to be found there and its radio call sign. A map reference should be accompanied by a brief description of the location, along with an estimated time of arrival of the rally car. The precise time allowed for servicing should be calculated and entered on the sheet, together with any fixed instructions such as changing from forest suspension to tarmac suspension, or a guide as to how much fuel is required. It should also include routine changes of major components like axles, gearboxes and suspension components – in such a way, it will be possible to make a good estimate of how much time will be available for unexpected repairs. The time of day should also be considered, allowing auxiliary lights to be fitted or removed as necessary.

This sheet should also detail how much time there is for each service crew to reach its next point and the distance to be travelled, together with route instructions. Depending entirely on individual needs, separate sheets could be drawn up for each service vehicle, or they could be lumped together on a main schedule, with each vehicle's instructions highlighted by using a flourescent marker pen. In any case, there should be a master schedule drawn up for the team manager's use.

Schedules can also be supplemented by maps (1:250 000 are best for this purpose) detailing the exact route for each vehicle and showing the location of garages where fuel can be taken on – especially service stations open 24 hours or automatic pumps which take one pound or five pound notes (making sure, of course, that the service crew has the necessary notes!). On the subject of money, each crew should be issued with a stock of cash to buy petrol and spares on the understanding that receipts are obtained. Finally, don't forget to thank your service crews after the rally; sometimes their job can be extremely anti-social.

The co-driver should draw up his own schedule to include amounts of fuel to be taken on at specific service points and which tyres should be fitted. When drawing up this table it should, of course, be remembered that the mileage figures should refer to the next section to be tackled, not the one just completed. A breakdown of road and stage mileage is essential in predicting fuel requirements and tyre choices.

Whenever possible, it helps to have a team briefing session, where schedules can be explained and mechanics can point out areas which need further clarification. Asking team members for their opinions at least shows you are interested in their thoughts, and if you show interest in them, they will likewise show interest in you. If you have a pre-event briefing, it never does any harm to follow it up after the rally with another session where mistakes can be analysed, with the possible view to writing a report and distributing it to each team member (to be treated in confidence) – it all helps to create the atmosphere of a proper team.

Team management is essential for the efficient running of any rally. Many of the items detailed previously may seem outlandishly extravagant for a small team, but when you analyse exactly what a co-driver does on any rally, it is a simple extension which can be applied to every event tackled. Take a close look at any large rally and you will see there are a number of separate smaller inter-team rallies taking place, where one team pits its managerial skills against another's. The practices detailed here really apply to Internationals, but with the exception of chase cars, they can be scaled down to fit any type of special stage rally.

13

Directory

Listed here are some useful contacts and addresses in the fields of rally organization, participation, preparation and education.

ORGANIZATIONS

RAC Motor Sports Association Ltd
31 Belgrave Square
London SW1X 8QH
(tel: 01-235 8601)

Royal Scottish Automobile Club
11 Blythswood Square
Glasgow G2 4AG
(tel: 041-221 3850)

Ulster Automobile Club
3 Botanic Avenue
Belfast BT7 1JG
(tel: 0232 618353)

Association of British International Rally Organizers
Stonelynk
Heathley End
Chislehurst
Kent
(tel: 0403 700220)

International Rally Drivers Club
Dilys Rogers
23 De Verdon Avenue
Belton
Loughborough
Leics
(tel: 0530 222958)

British Trials and Rally Drivers Association Ltd
Mrs S.R. Knight

8 Beechwood Road
Easton in Gordano
Bristol BS20 0NA
(tel: 027-581 3772)

British Rally Marshal's Club
Mrs A. Hemingway
5 Pinfold Close
Lound
Nr Retford
Notts DN22 8SJ
(tel: 0777 818527)

REGIONAL ASSOCIATIONS

Central Southern (ACSMC)
Tim Walton
2 Shaldon Way
Calthorpe Park
Fleet
Hants GU13 8ET
(tel: 025-14 29446)

Midland (AMMC)
D. Lucas
29 Avondale Close
Kingswinford
Dudley
West Midlands
(tel: 0384 271543)

North East Midlands (ANEMMC)
J.B. Wilkinson
1 Bayons Avenue
Springfield
Grimsby
South Humberside DN33 3LN
(tel: 0472 59232)

Eastern (AEMC)
A.C. Nisbett
8 Woodside Lane
Bexley
Kent DA5 1JL
(tel: 01-303 0654)

North East and Cumbria (ANECC)
Bill Troughear
Arragon House
Hornsby Gate
Headsnook
Carlisle
(tel: 076-886 603)

Northern (ANCC)
J.H. Richardson
67 West Park
Selby
North Yorks YO8 0JN
(tel: 0757 702048)

Northern Ireland (ANICC)
N. Moffitt
7 Malone Park
Kilfennan
Londonderry BT47 1PE
(tel: 0504 41928)

South Eastern (ASEMC)
D. Webb
Clearways
St Johns Road
Bexhill-on-Sea
East Sussex
(tel: 0424 225568)

West Midlands (AWMMC)
R.W. Griffiths
Nodstock
Alberbury
Shrewsbury SY5 9AD
(tel: 074-378 472)

East of Scotland (ESACC)
R.P. Grimwood
20 Drum Brae Place
Edinburgh 12
(tel: 031-339 7279)

North Western (ANWCC)
A. Dean-Lewis
44 Penrhyn Isaf Road
Llandudno
North Wales
(tel: 0492 46688)

South Western (ASWMC)
R.B. Mayo
88 Queensholm Drive
Downend
Bristol
(tel: 0272 560114)

West Scotland (AWSMSC)
D. Attwood
Jura
Larg Road
Stranraer
(tel: 0776 4791)

East Midlands (EMAMC)
Val Shenton
25 Wells Road
Mickleover
Derby DE3 5BU
(tel: 0332 513940)

London Counties (LCAMC)
A. Biss
6 Wavertree Road
South Woodford
London E18
(tel: 01-989 2515)

Welsh (WAMC)
Ron Summerfield
Llyswen
20 Three Elms Road
Hereford HR4 0RH
(tel: 0432 273409)

EQUIPMENT MANUFACTURERS AND SUPPLIERS

Terratrip
Ship Farm
Horsley Road
Horsley
Derby DE2 5BR
(tel: 0332 880468)
[Manufacturers of tripmeters and watches]

Rally Navigation Services
20 Sherwood Avenue
Layton
Blackpool
(tel: 0253 37976)
[Suppliers of navigation equipment, maps and books]

Ripspeed International
418-426 Hertford Road
Edmonton
London N9
(tel: 01-805 4711)
[Suppliers of Rallycom intercoms]

Road and Racing Accessories Ltd
75-77 Moore Park Road
Fulham
London SW6 2HH
(tel: 01-736 2881)
[Suppliers of Peltor intercoms]

Sonic Helmets Ltd
202 Bradford Road
Castle Bromwich
Birmingham B36 9AA
(tel: 021-749 4900)
[Manufacturers of Sonic intercoms and helmets]

Halda Ltd
4 Brandon Road
York Way
London N7 9AE
(tel: 01-607 1207)
[Suppliers of Halda tripmeters]

Lucas Industries Ltd
Competition Department
Great Hampton Street
Birmingham B18
(tel: 021-236 5055)
[Manufacturers of lighting and electrical
equipment]

Hella Automotive Equipment
Daventry Road Industrial Estate
Banbury
Oxon OX16 7JU
(tel: 0295 56381)
[Manufacturers of lighting and electrical
equipment]

Don Barrow
4 Sandy Lane
Whirley
Macclesfield
Cheshire
[Manufacturers of map magnifiers and romers]

NAVIGATING/CO-DRIVING COURSES

Ian Hughes Rally School
Castle Garage
Conwy
North Wales
(tel: 049-263 6435)

Bill Gwynne Rally School
Station House Works
Westbury
Brackley
Northants
(tel: 0295 710028)